British Clocks Illustrated

Books by Brian Loomes include:

Grandfather Clocks & their Cases
Complete British Clocks
White Dial Clocks, the complete guide
Country Clocks & their London Origins
The Early Clockmakers of Great Britain
Yorkshire Clockmakers
Lancashire Clocks & Clockmakers
Westmorland Clocks & Clockmakers
Watchmakers & Clockmakers of the World, Vol. 2
Clocks – guide to dating & valuation
Antique British Clocks – A Buyer's Guide

British Clocks Illustrated

Brian Loomes

ROBERT HALE · LONDON

First published in Great Britain 1992

ISBN 0 7090 4547 6

Robert Hale Limited
Clerkenwell House
Clerkenwell Green
London EC1R 0HT

Photoset by
Derek Doyle & Associates, Mold, Clwyd.
Printed and bound in Hong Kong
by Bookbuilders Ltd.

Contents

Preface	7
1 Lantern clocks	9
2 Longcase clocks	67
Thirty-hour brass dials	
Eight-day brass dials	
White dials	
3 Tavern clocks	199
4 Bracket clocks	207
5 Spring wall clocks	245
Glossary	259
Select bibliography	266
Index	269

PHOTOGRAPHS

The photographs in this book are almost entirely of clocks the author has handled as a dealer over the years. The photographs were taken by the author and his son, Robert Loomes. They were processed and printed by the author's wife, Joy Loomes, and his son, Robert Loomes.

Preface

This book is intended as a pictorial survey of the types and styles of clocks made in Britain from the beginnings in about 1600 until the trade was swamped with imported clocks in the mid-nineteenth century. Some Scottish, Welsh and Irish clocks are included, but stylistic developments do, of course, apply to clocks made throughout the British Isles.

The book is laid out in such a way that all information relating to a particular example appears alongside the illustration. It is hoped that this system will aid the novice in identifying his clock, as well as those with more experience who wish to add to their knowledge of this fascinating subject. The large format photographs should also be of particular interest to restorers, whose need is for clear illustrations. Technical information has been kept to a minimum to avoid overwhelming the beginner. Any technical or unfamiliar term not explained in the text will be found in the glossary.

At the time of writing, no other clock book follows this pattern. I hope the reader will find it useful and will be encouraged to delve further into the history of clocks.

Brian Loomes
Pateley Bridge
1991

1 *Lantern clocks*

For all practical purposes, the lantern clock can be assumed to have begun in England in about the year 1600. It was the first native British domestic clock. A handful exist that were made before that date, either brought to this country by foreign workmen or made in this country by them. The term lantern clock is a recent one. At the time, they were referred to simply as clocks or sometimes as brass clocks. Occasionally the term Cromwellian clock was used, but as these clocks were by no means confined to Cromwell's time, that term is little used today, and is frowned upon by collectors.

In the early years, the lantern clockmaking industry was small and almost exclusively located in London. Because of this, and because of sheer wastage through the centuries, examples of lantern clocks met with today seldom date from before the mid-seventeenth century. They do exist, though they are very uncommon. A further reason for this scarcity is that these clocks became obsolete because pendulum-controlled clocks were more accurate, and it was not uncommon for them to be traded in for their scrap-metal value when a newer, more efficient clock was purchased. Those that survive have often been modified to the newer pendulum-control systems. Those that have survived unaltered have often done so because they were abandoned disused for many years.

The first lantern clocks were controlled by the balance-wheel system, having a circular wheel which swung to and fro to enforce timekeeping. Regulation of timekeeping was imposed by adding or removing lead shot from a weight canister, and was to some extent a matter of trial and error. Temperature affected the timekeeping; balance-wheel lantern clocks were inclined to be erratic, and are said to have varied by as much as a quarter of an hour a day. It is probably for this reason that lantern clocks mark the time in units of a quarter of an hour, registered by a single hand. A few do exist with two hands, but most of those are in fact single-handers which have been altered to two hands later.

Lantern clocks built originally with two hands are extremely uncommon.

The introduction of the pendulum in 1658 brought a much more efficient timekeeping control, by use of the verge escapement and short bob pendulum. Within a very few years the long pendulum with anchor escapement was introduced, probably during the 1670s though the date is disputed by various authorities. The availability of these two improved timekeeping controls within this very short space of time meant that original balance-wheel lantern clocks were usually converted to short or long pendulum. Very few balance-wheel clocks survive with balance-wheel control, and most surviving balance-wheel clocks today have been restored to the balance-wheel system by enthusiasts. To distinguish one from the other, collectors usually refer to 'original balance-wheel' or 'reconverted balance-wheel'.

The verge escapement models with short bob pendulums seldom survive in unaltered form, as most were modified to the long pendulum and anchor escapement (sometimes known as the Royal pendulum). This was often done within a very few years of the clock's making, to bring it into more efficient use. Some verge models have been converted back to the original form in recent years, and collectors distinguish between them by referring to 'original verge' or 'reconverted verge'. In the illustrations of lantern clocks which follow, an attempt has been made to clarify what form of escapement the clock was built with, and whether the escapement the clock now has is original or a later modification.

Alterations of escapement would be regarded as a serious defect from a collector's point of view today in some clocks where alteration was unusual, long case clocks, for example. In lantern clocks, however, such conversions to improved escapement forms tend to be regarded as almost inevitable, and stand as a record of the history of that clock's passage through time.

To the newcomer, lantern clocks all look very much alike. With a little experience, however, considerable variation in styling can be seen, most noticeably with the progression of styling over the years. The overall similarity which seems apparent at first in a clock of 1650 and one of 1700, stems no doubt from the fact that the lantern clock trade was practised by relatively few craftsmen originally, and as those skills were passed down through apprentices over two or more generations, the master would pass something of his own personal style to his successor. Nevertheless, styles do change gradually in a pattern which can be recognized, and the illustrations attempt to draw attention to this stylistic development.

Most lantern clocks were hung from a sturdy hook in the wall, by means of an iron hoop at the back of the clock. They were held off the wall in a vertical plane by two iron spikes at the lower rear, known as spurs. The spurs were often set into the back feet of the clock.

Alongside true lantern clocks, there existed another, more simplified version of a hanging wall clock, often known today as a hook-and-spike wall clock. This was usually a rural clock such as might be made by a blacksmith or country metal worker, often known as a clocksmith. A hook-and-spike clock often made much greater use of iron than brass, iron costing only one tenth the price of brass. Examples of these clocks are shown amongst the illustrations.

Hooded clocks were another form of hanging wall clock which in essence developed from a lantern/hook-and-spike principle. The clock was set on a wall shelf and had its movement enclosed in a box-like hood to keep out dust. Hooded clocks began as post-framed clocks, but later examples often occur in plated form.

1. A rare relic being the dial from a very early lantern clock dated 1627. Only the dial survives. The initials RK at the top centre may be the maker (in which case he is unrecorded) or the first owner. Note the crude cherub-head decoration and the primitive nature of the engraving in general. On these very early clocks the half hours are marked by asterisks and quarter hours are not marked at all – though they always were later. The blank centre area would originally have been covered by an alarm disc, and no care was taken to prevent the engraved ruling out lines from straying into this zone as it would have been hidden. The hole in the chapter ring between X and XI is where the alarm pivot once was. A clock of this date must have had balance-wheel control.

2. Standard-size lantern clock (about 15ins, 40 cms) of typical form, made in the 1640s and signed on the front fret 'William Sellwood at ye marmayde in Lothbury' – indicating that he worked at the sign of the Mermaid in Lothbury, London. Originally a balance-wheel clock, converted later to anchor. The blank central zone would originally have been covered by an engraved alarm disc. The chapter ring is of the early narrow type. The heavy single hand could well be original. Note right-hand hammer, shield pattern frets and heavy finials of early pattern. Close-clustered flower pattern inside chapter ring is an early feature.

3. This lantern clock is unsigned, as many were. It dates from the 1660s and may be the work of Nicholas Coxeter of London. The Tudor Rose engraving of the alarm disc is typical of the period, as is the close-clustered floral engraving to the dial centre, here based on tulips. The dolphin frets, heavy finials and narrow chapter ring are all early features. The iron hand is believed original. This clock was a verge pendulum between split trains, converted later to anchor escapement. In this example the hammer positioned on the right indicates that it had a separate weight each for going and striking trains. Standard height of 15 ins (40 cms).

4. The dial-sheet of the anonymous (?Coxeter) clock (3) is here seen removed and shows the four chapter-ring feet and their method of pinning. The dial is here upside down and the location lug at the top pins into the bottom of the frame when assembled. This dial is made from an old church brass memorial inscription dating from almost a hundred years earlier. The words 'lyeth bin … (beneath)' and 'of London' can be seen clearly. The newer ring of brass around the centre hole shows where the dial-sheet has been bushed to take up wear. Note the filing of the dial-sheet edge for a snug fit.

5. An intriguing standard-size lantern clock, originally balance wheel but, like most others, converted later to anchor. The maker's name could be Edmund Aston, or he might be Edmund, of a place named Aston; in either case, his name is not recorded, nor is it known which Aston, though the clock has several West Country features, such as the fact that the finials, pillars and feet are constructed in one piece. In most regions these were in three parts screwed together. The clock could date from the 1640 to 1660 period. An alarm disc originally covered the centre zone, the alarm work pivot hole showing between X and XI. Finials and feet are of bold early pattern, and the shield-centre fret is also often early. The iron hand could be original. Right-hand hammer here indicates a former balance wheel. Side doors missing. Tiny half-hour markers are usually an early sign.

6. Standard-sized lantern clock by the only clockmaker in Scotland known to have made lantern clocks, Humphrey Mills or Milne of Edinburgh, his name being spelt either way. The style has many features suggestive of a very early period – close-clustered flower centre, heavy finials, shield frets, split-turned feet, and right-hand hammer (indicating it was originally a balance-wheel clock). Other features such as the half-hour marker, suggest the clock is a little later. However, Mills is not known to have worked in Edinburgh before about 1660, and the clock is tentatively dated to the 1660s. It is possible he was working in an archaic style, or even that he bought the clocks in and simply signed his name on the fret, as the name engraving is very crude, whilst the dial centre is very fine. The hand looks original despite its not having the usual heavy pointer. Could Mills have been selling clocks in the 1660s that were already twenty years old?

7. Lantern clock of standard size by London maker Thomas Knifton who worked at the sign of the Cross Keys in Lothbury. Originally a balance-wheel clock dating from the 1650s, this was later modified to anchor escapement and further modified to take a minute hand. The dial can be seen to be calibrated for a single hand only. The blank dial centre together with traces of the (filled) hole between X and XI are indications that it originally had alarm work. Anchor conversion often necessitated the removal of alarm work, which was in the way of the long pendulum (outside the backplate). The hour hand could be original, as it has the typical tail of a single hand, yet it looks unusually delicate. By this time the finial pattern is becoming more elongated. Dolphin frets, as this pattern is known, were popular over a long period. The trident pattern half-hour marker developed before long into a full-blown fleur-de-lis of heavier proportion as chapter rings grew wider.

8. Standard-size lantern clock signed 'Will Raynes in Yorke', a maker who trained in London, but worked in York from the later 1670s till he died in 1695 upon falling from his horse. This clock appears to date from the 1690s and was made with anchor escapement. Many stylistic features place this towards the end of the century – wider chapter ring with heavier fleur-de-lis half-hour marker, more scrolling centre engraving, though still harking back to the tulip/daisy themes of twenty years before. The iron hand could be original. The elongated finial shape tends to indicate this period but the rounded feet which were a pattern used over a long period are not especially useful as a period indicator. Very few lantern clocks seem to be preserved from York or Yorkshire, and this type of clock was apparently far less popular in the north than in the south-east and London.

9. Standard-sized lantern clock of typical form (15ins, 40cms), seen here in unrestored condition. It was made about 1690 by George Guest of Aston, Birmingham. The front fret has the lion and unicorn motif, a design found most often in the West Country. Fleurs-de-lis half-hour markers are typical of this period. The steel hand is original and pitted with rust. The shapes of feet and finials vary somewhat from maker to maker. Note the front right finial is a replacement fitted carelessly on top of the broken stump of the original. The side doors are missing, a common fault, as they simply pushed into place and were often lost. Finials, pillars and feet are made in a single casting, and this is also a feature most often found in the West Country. The dial-centre engraving is of a particularly delicate nature, illustrating the style of the individual engraver.

10. View looking down from the back of a standard-size lantern clock of about 1690 with original verge escapement, showing verge wheel (or crown wheel as it is sometimes called), verge staff, pendulum, and retaining clip. The semi-circular iron hoop by which it would have hung from the wall, shows well. The countwheel can also be seen; this was the striking system employed by virtually all thirty-hour clocks, both lantern and longcase. The iron backplate, here removed, would normally conceal everything inside the frame and would help to keep it dust-free. This clock can be seen to be in dusty condition. The maker of this clock was Francis Stamper of London.

11. Standard-size lantern clock of about 1690 signed 'James Delaunce In Froome fecit'. This maker worked in Frome, Somerset, between about 1685 and 1695. The finials, pillars and feet are cast in one piece in the style associated mostly with Bristol, but these feet and finials are of unusual pattern and quite splendid in their originality of design. The lion and unicorn fret is also a regular West Country feature. This clock was probably built with anchor escapement, but the movement has been totally replaced much later, probably in Victorian times, by a spring-driven double-fusee movement, as can be seen by the two winding-holes cut into the dial centre. A clock converted in this way to spring-drive is much less valuable than one with its original movement, but it is nevertheless an interesting relic and quite collectable, especially one with such fine style as this. The blank dial centre would once have had an alarm disc – notice the practice engraving of a small flower below 'fecit', which would have been hidden by the alarm disc originally.

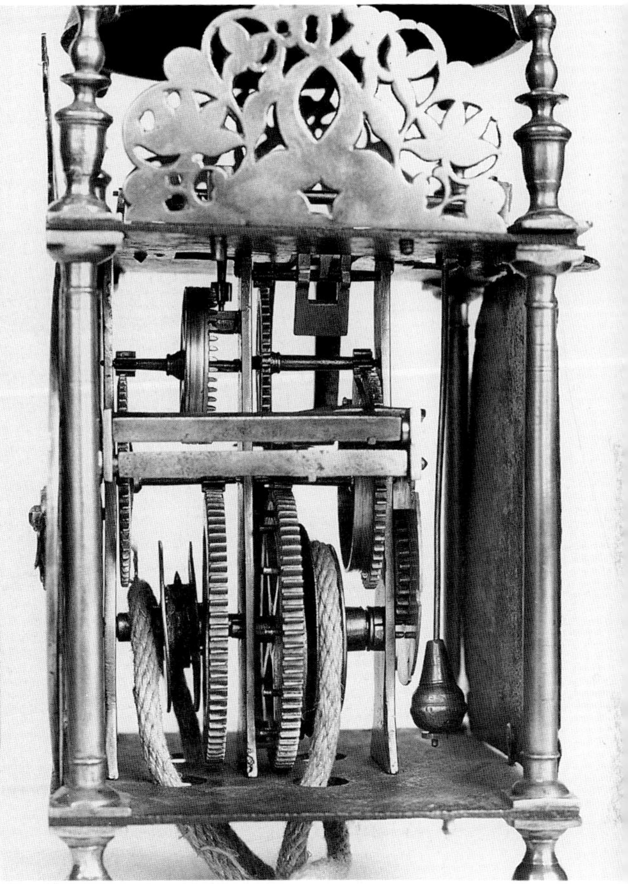

12. A standard-size lantern clock signed and dated 1692, made by Richard Savage of Shrewsbury and believed to be the oldest surviving Shrewsbury clock to have yet come to light. It retains its original verge escapement. An unusual feature indicative of the maker's personal taste is that the top and bottom plates are of iron and show dark in the photograph – normally these are of brass. The names 'Edw. Mill. Pardo' are engraved on the top fret, which research proved to be Edward and Milborough Pardo, a local couple who married that year, and the clock was almost certainly made as a wedding present probably purchased for them by parents. The asterisk half-hour marker is an archaic stylistic feature more often found sixty or more years earlier. It is most unusual to find a clock with a known date of origin and ownership. The iron hand is believed original.

13. The movement of the clock by Richard Savage (12) showing the verge escapement with the pendulum positioned unusually *inside* the backplate. The side doors have been removed for this photograph. The contrate wheel with its decorative scored ringing can be seen clearly as can the shaped wheel collets, which are of iron and integral with the arbors. Notice the dolphin side frets lack any engraving, which was normal treatment for many side frets. The tip of the iron hanging hoop can just be seen protruding behind the right finial base. The iron top and bottom plates can be seen to contrast against the brass of the finials, pillars and feet.

James
Ogden

15. Detail of the iron bell strap from the James Ogden lantern clock (14). The decorative four-holed pattern at the finial base is also found on some conventional brass bell straps. The negative strap endings are cut to wrap round the clock's corner finials instead of the usual method of plugging into them with a pin. Note the crack in the bell! Note also that the bell-strap finial does not match the corner ones in plate 14, and this could be a replacement. The movement of this clock was built with a short verge pendulum between the trains, known as a split-trains type, but was long ago converted to anchor escapement, as most such were.

14. Standard-size lantern clock made by James Ogden of Soyland, near Halifax, an early Quaker clockmaker whose clocks are scarce. Lantern clocks are especially unusual from Yorkshire. This has heavy, bold engraving, and the wider chapter ring with heavy fleur-de-lis half-hour markers are all indicative of the end of the seventeenth century. The dial-centre retains the Tudor Rose influence and the tulip theme. The unusual iron hand is believed original. The frets are of floral pattern, though here the front one, which is not engraved, is unusual, as normally only side frets are left plain; yet they are believed to be original. Note the casting flaw in the chapter ring above the X in XII. The bell strap here is of iron, very unusual, though original. This clock is full of character and individuality and very different from London work of the day.

16. A fine large lantern clock of about 1690, standing 17½ ins (47 cms) high, unsigned, as many were, and almost certainly of London origin. It is pictured here in unrestored condition and lacks the side doors and the two side frets. The front fret is preserved and bears the engraved initials BL in its centre – perhaps those of the original owner. The feet and finials are unusually big. The steel hand, slightly rust-pitted, is original, as is the alarm disc, though the alarm work itself was removed when converted to long pendulum, as was commonly the case, since the alarm work occupied the space needed for the pendulum. The Tudor Rose theme dominates the centre (on the alarm disc), but towards the end of the century the floral centre sometimes takes a wreath-like form, as here. The chapter ring is 7 ins (17 cms) in diameter and 1½ ins wide (3.5 cms).

17. A handsome lantern clock made in the 1690s by Richard Martin of Northampton. The clock is of standard size (15 ins, 40 cms) and of traditional form. However, the presence of two hands (on a single-handed dial) and of two winding-holes cut through the engraved pattern, indicate that this clock was converted later to a two-handed spring-driven movement. Everything external dates from the late seventeenth century; everything inside probably from the late nineteenth. The two hands are replacements of 'Gothic' appearance but late nineteenth century. Similar conversion to spring-drive and thus table-top use took place on many such clocks, at a time when they were otherwise regarded as obsolete and might have been scrapped. The lettering of the maker's name is here very cramped as the chapter ring overlaps it slightly – suggesting that the dial-sheet and chapter ring may have been the work of two people. Or perhaps that the clockmaker made do with the size he happened to have ready.

18. Lantern clock made in the 1690s by Abraham Farrer, a maker who is known to have worked at Pontefract by the 1690s, though the clock might just possibly have been made before he went there. The style has certain affinities with the work of the Halifax Ogdens. The bell strap is of iron and of negative fitting, like that on the James Ogden clock (14). The chapter ring is boldly engraved, often a northern feature. In this clock the top and bottom movement plates are of iron (most are brass), an unusual practice and indicative of individual workmanship. The pillars are turned in one with the finials and feet, a most unusual practice in the north and a feature usually associated with West Country makers. The hand is believed to be a replacement. The naïve engraved cherub face above VI is a theme of some lantern clocks. The closely engraved wrigglework flowers are of a strange style occasionally met with and done in such a way as to have a comic look to them, and are also associated with the West Country.

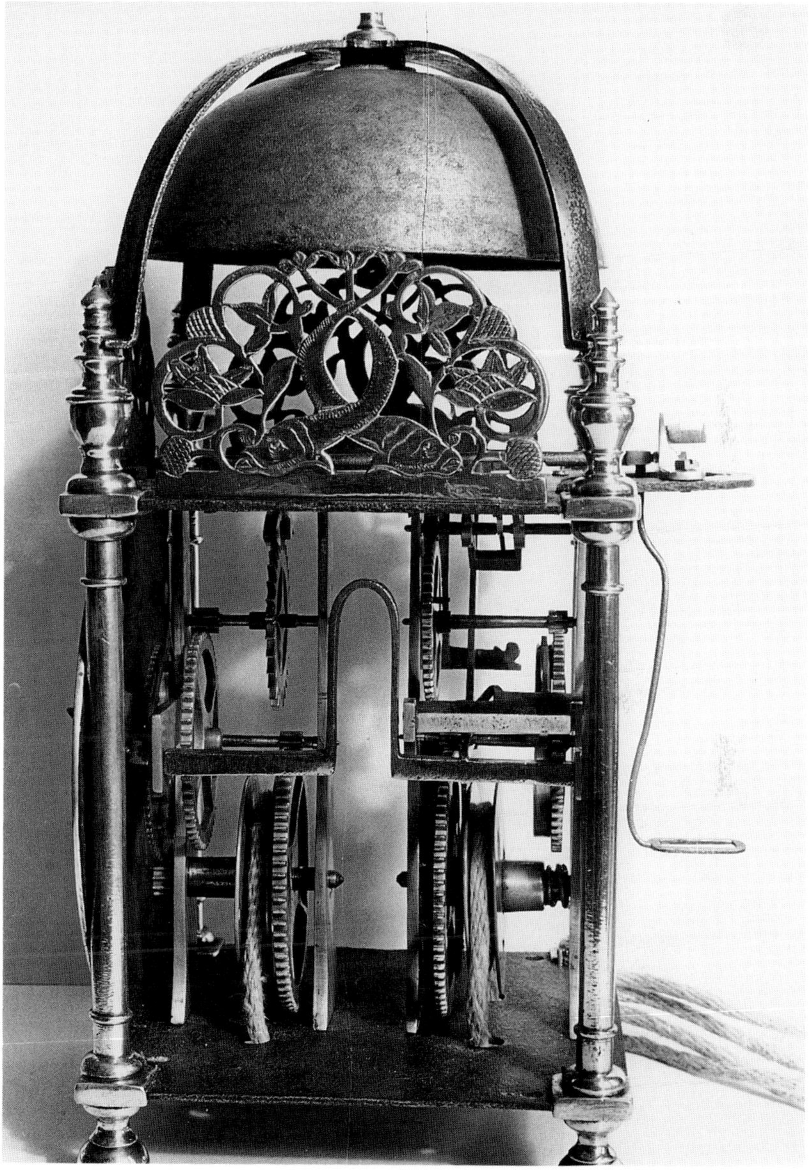

19. Movement of the lantern clock by Abraham Farrer made in the 1690s. This can be seen to be of the split-trains type, which must originally have been a verge pendulum. Note the arch in the strikework detent, made this way to avoid the centre-swinging bob pendulum. This clock was converted, long ago, to anchor escapement. The original hanging hoop is preserved, now used as a base for the pendulum back cock. The spurs have disappeared, as have the side doors. The iron top and bottom plates fit at the corners into slots in the pillars, each corner being held by a pin on the inside.

20. Typical London lantern clock of the 1680s of standard size made by Thomas Bradford of London. The floral centre is typical of the time, a space being left for the name below XII. The blued steel hand is believed original. The half-hour markers are more restrained than some northern ones. The construction of finials, pillars and feet in three separate sections is normal for London. The frets are of the heraldic type, carrying a centre shield surrounded by scrollwork including acorns. Some shields carry the initials of the first owner. The position of the hammer on the left (it can be seen behind the fret) indicates that the movement has continuous rope drive (some are chain), and this normally means the movement will have either verge or anchor escapement – here a verge pendulum.

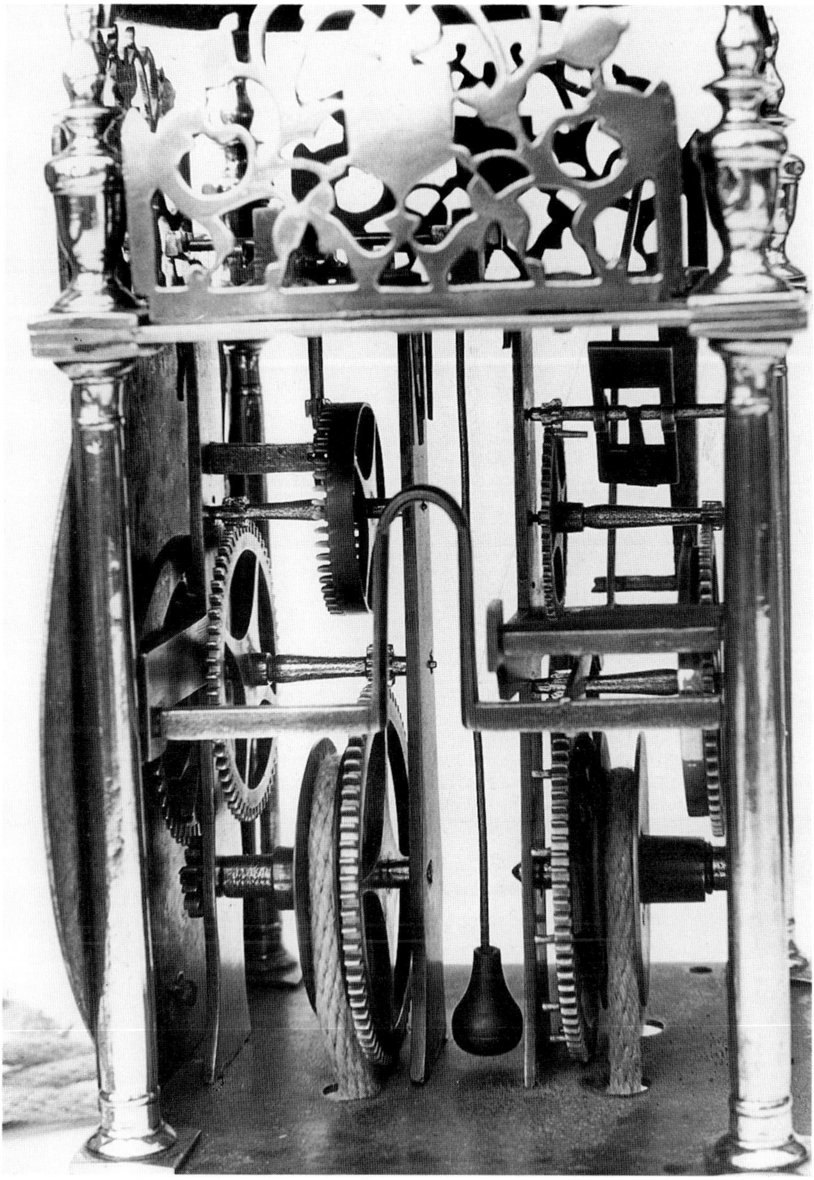

21. Movement of the lantern clock by Thomas Bradford of London (20), with its original verge escapement and bob pendulum. This one has the pendulum between the trains – known as the split-trains type or divided trains. Many have been converted later to anchor escapement, but the divided trains make an unmistakable recognition feature and any such clock must originally have been built with verge pendulum. Notice that the wheel arbors are especially well-shaped, a feature much liked by collectors. Not surprisingly, the pinions show considerable wear, especially the fly pinion.

22. Smaller sized lantern clock just under 9 ins high (22.5 cms) with chapter ring of 4 ins in diameter (10 cms), made about 1700 by Simon de Charmes of London, who was of French origin. This is a non-striking clock with alarm work, known as an alarm timepiece. These were more often made in smaller form than striking ones, as they were used as travelling alarms and were easier carried in this smaller size. Note the use of meeting arrowheads for half-hour markers (and also on the alarm disc); these are usually a sign of the style of the new century. The dolphin frets look crude alongside the other engraving, and may be replacements. The name fills most of the available dial centre on these smaller clocks, leaving little room for decorative engraving. The top finial is a replacement, differing in shape from the others. The feet appear bent, but in fact both feet and finials are made on a twist pattern, a deliberate feature of the making, yet an oddity of style not usually met with. The steel hand appears original.

23. Movement of the travelling alarm lantern clock by Simon de Charmes of London (22) with original verge escapement. The pull-wind ratchet and click can be seen, well-filed to take chain drive, the chain being off its ratchet in the picture. The alarm work is attached to the inside of the backplate. Its chain is removed in this picture, but the two holes in the baseplate show where it runs. Note the spurs protruding from the rear feet and the hoop at the back of the top plate. The pear-shaped bob is typical in shape and has decorative rings scribed round, a common practice. Notice that by this time the arbors tend to be less shapely than earlier, especially on these smaller clocks. The side doors are removed for the photograph. Notice the repair to the right-hand spur of the bell strap.

24. Standard-sized lantern clock of about 1700 by Henry Mayhew of Parham, Suffolk, seen here in unrestored condition. Meeting arrowhead half-hour markers are typical of the beginning of the eighteenth century. The chapter rings are now noticeably wider than on earlier examples. The original spurs can just be seen behind the back feet. This scroll engraving style of centre is typical of the period. The lion and unicorn fret is more often associated with the West Country. The original hand has a replacement tip, which gives it an incorrect appearance. The clock was originally a verge escapement, converted later to anchor. The placing of the signature on the chapter ring rather than the dial centre occurs from this date on, seldom earlier.

25. Standard-sized lantern clock with square dial 8 ins high by 7½ ins wide (20 cms by 19 cms) made by John Mason of London about 1715. By now the dial had become similar to a small longcase dial, with spandrels and the matted-centre styling of a longcase dial. The blued steel hand is a replacement based on contemporary examples. The meeting arrowhead half-hour markers are typical of the early century. The clock has hoop-and-spurs and a verge pendulum outside the backplate. The square-dial version of the lantern clock was unusual in London, a passing fashion; though in the provinces makers felt free to do as they wished, and this style is probably more often seen there. The frets appear to be original and interestingly the front one is engraved only on that part that shows above the dial top. By the time this square-dial lantern clock appeared in London, the lantern clock was fading as a genre.

26. Miniature travelling alarm with arched dial dating from about 1720, the maker William Webster of Exchange Alley, London. The dial is about 6 ins high (15 cms) and 4 ins wide (10 cms), total height with top finial 7 ins (17 cms). This is still a sort of lantern clock, with finials, feet, and hoop-and-spurs for wall-hanging, and from this time forward travelling alarm-clocks often had this shape of dial. The dial is much like a tiny longcase clock in style. Diamond-shaped half-hour markers (sometimes called lozenge-shaped) are a feature of some clocks of this period. The matted dial centre often became an alternative to the earlier engraved centres. The hand is of blued steel and is believed to be original.

27. Internal view of the William Webster alarm timepiece (26), the side doors have been removed for the photograph. The verge escapement can be seen clearly on the right. The alarm work is attached to the inside of the backplate (on the left). Bell strap, side frets, finials and feet all show well. The original hoop can be seen on the upper left, and the spurs in the rear feet, lower left. Note the engraved rings decorating the pendulum bob.

28. View of the William Webster travelling alarm (26) from the rear. The iron backplate shows clearly, the rivet points being the attachments carrying the alarm work inside the backplate. The hoop is below the pendulum support by the top plate; the spurs can be seen screwed behind the rear feet. The side doors are back in place for this photograph. The bell is for the alarm work, as such clocks do not strike the hours, the double-headed alarm hammer can be seen on its staff immediately below the bell lip. Notice the handmade screws showing behind the dial sheet, which hold the spandrels in place. This particular example is rope-driven, whereas some had a chain. Either option was available, but chain was fractionally more costly when new.

29. Mid-eighteenth-century lantern clock of the 'Turkish Market' type, made for export to the Middle East and having pseudo-Turkish numbering. Henton Brown was working from 1726 till his death in 1775. Total height of the clock is 15 ins (40 cms). This is still a true lantern clock but with an arched dial as with most Turkish market examples. Note the crescent theme worked into the spandrels, a pattern only used for these export models. The clock has original verge pendulum, which was almost always used on Turkish models for ease of transportation. The matted dial centre and original steel hands are typical of the period, when conventional London lantern clocks were virtually obsolete. This clock would hang from a hook on the wall, though some were on wall brackets. These later examples are normally two-handers, as here. Half a dozen London makers dominated the Turkish market in clocks.

30. Side view of the Henton Brown lantern clock (29), the doors removed for this photograph. Note the finials, feet and side frets, typical features of a true lantern clock. The frets are basically the dolphin pattern but have crescents engraved on them to adapt them for this custom. By this time the wheel arbors are plain and without the earlier taper. Steelwork too is undecorated. The pendulum hangs outside the backplate (of brass on these later models – iron earlier); note the pear-shaped bob, typical of many verge bobs.

31. Side view of the Henton Brown lantern clock (29) with doors in place, each engraved with a crescent theme. The hanging hoop shows well here, but the spurs are missing – a hole can be seen in each of the rear feet where they formerly screwed into place. The bell strap system is exactly the same in principle as on earlier lanterns, even though on these arched dial models it is largely hidden from the front. The feet on lantern clocks are sometimes called 'pendants', since in normal use when the clock was hung by its hoop-and-spurs, these would be no more than decorative inverted finials. When such clocks were placed on wall brackets, they did serve the function of feet, which is the term most commonly used to describe them.

32. A highly ornate and eccentric Turkish Market lantern clock made in about 1750 by Richard Peckover of London, pictured here in unrestored condition. This *is* a lantern clock, but its box-like casing has become so ornate in style as to completely enclose it. Even the bell is hidden inside the dome-like top-piece. The chapter ring, original steel hand and matted dial centre are all that remain of typical nature. Every other feature is quite un-typical and perhaps even unique. The height is about 15 ins (40 cms). The movement has a verge pendulum and is, of course, weight-driven, but the overall appearance has become much more like a bracket clock. This is a measure of the lengths to which some makers would go to adopt what they felt would be an appealing style to suit the intended market.

33. Typical arched-dial lantern clock of standard size and dating from about 1760-70. The dial style is much like a longcase dial of the day, but in miniature. The clock is photographed in unrestored condition. The hand is of the right size and style, but is made of brass and is very thin and probably a replacement. Spandrels and centre engraving are similar to those on contemporary longcase clocks, but in smaller format. The maker is William Shaw of Bottesdale in Suffolk. These arched-dial lanterns were often signed on a circular plate in the arch, as here. Diamond or lozenge half-hour markers were sometimes used on longcase dials, but more often on arched dial lantern clocks. The dial size is 10 ins by 7 ins (25.5 cms by 17 cms); chapter ring 6 ins in diameter (15 cms).

34. The movement of the William Shaw of Bottesdale arched-dial lantern clock (33) shows that it was originally constructed with split trains for centre verge pendulum (later converted to anchor). This was an old-fashioned system when the clock was made, but probably retained in use because the short pendulum was self-contained within the clock and made it more easily portable. The clock has original finials, but the feet have been cut short (probably so that it will stand on a shelf more easily) and the frets it once had are now missing. The bell is attached by a bell stand in the same manner as a longcase clock. The typical lantern-clock bell-strap system was largely hidden by an arched dial, which may be why it was not used here. Generally, a bell stand is stronger and a more sensible construction. This sort of lantern clock represents the end of the fashion; hooded clocks or hook-and-spike clocks did the same job more satisfactorily, and more cheaply.

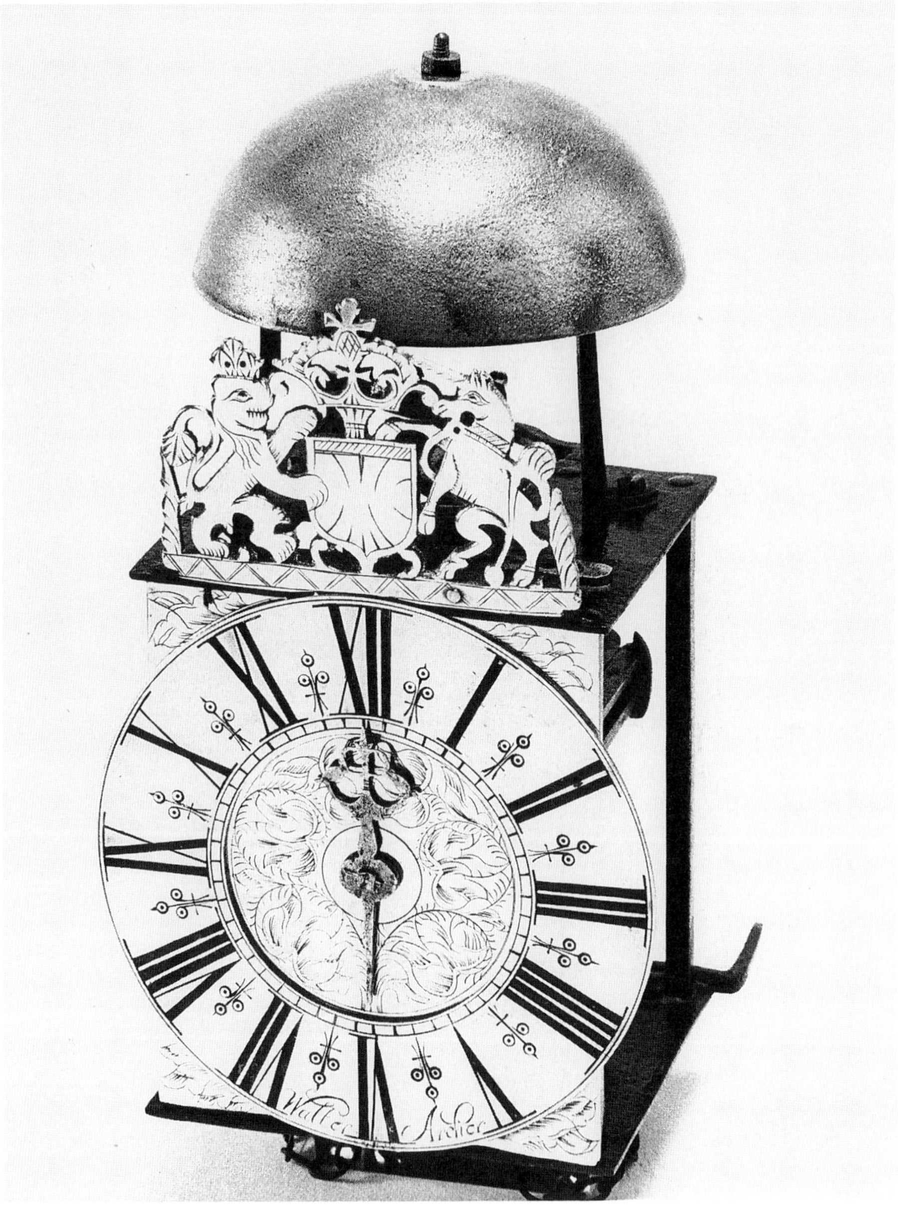

35. A very interesting hanging wall clock made about 1710-20 by Walter Archer, who worked, at least after about 1714, at Stow-on-the-Wold. The clock is entirely original, including the steel hand (slightly rust-pitted). However it represents a transitional stage, being half lantern and half hook-and-spike wall clock. The dial-sheet, chapter ring, front fret and dial-centre engraving style are all typical of a contemporary lantern clock. Everything behind the dial is much more typical of a hook-and-spike wall clock. Overall height about 13 ins (33 cms). Archer's work is easily recognized by his own personal styling, seen in the dial-centre pattern, his particular form of the lion-and-unicorn fret, and, most obvious of all, his unusual half-hour markers consisting of a fleur-de-lis of three dotted circles. A very unusual hybrid form of clock, rarely seen, yet illustrative of the origin of the one form from the other in principle.

36. Rear view of the Walter Archer transitional lantern clock (35). The top and bottom plates are of iron. The bell stand is of the normal longcase type, though the hammer still strikes on the inside of the bell, lantern fashion. In this photograph the bell has been removed to allow sight of the original anchor escapement. This clock never had side frets or side doors. The original hanging hoop can be seen riveted to the top plate, and the original spurs to the lower plate. The spurs are spread wide apart to allow the long pendulum ample clearance between them. This movement is more akin to a post-framed longcase movement than a true lantern one. Note the original wooden weight pulley, a little chipped with use.

37. Unsigned hook-and-spike wall clock with 6½ ins (16 cms) square dial. This is a primitive yet charming clock, possibly Quaker-made – the lack of signature and the spandrels and ring-turned centre decoration are all features sometimes used by Quaker makers. The 'spandrels' are brass studs. Lozenge half-hour markers were favoured by some Quakers as being less fussy than fleur-de-lis for example. The iron hand is original. Such a clock is difficult to date with any certainty. My estimate is between 1710 and 1720. This is a fully-fledged hook-and-spike wall clock, a wall-hung timepiece alarm (no strikework). They were much cheaper to make than lantern clocks and served the same function for a cottage owner. They are not commonplace items today, especially examples of this great age.

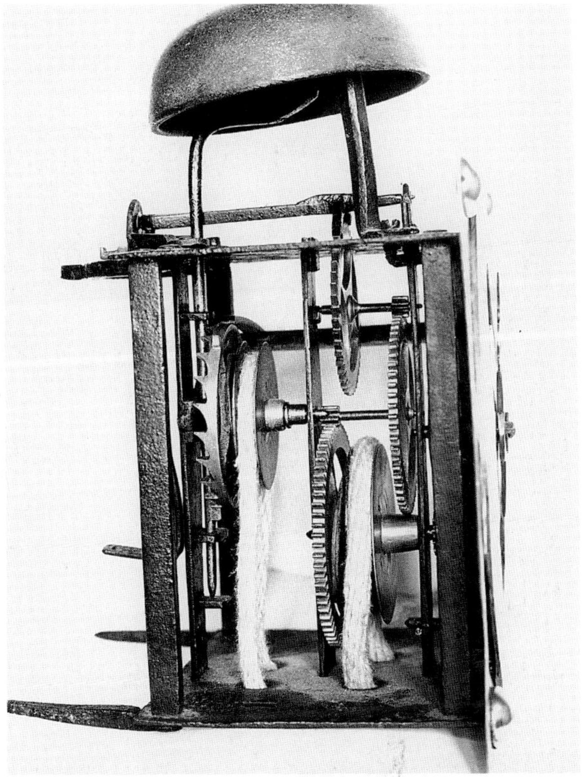

38. Side view of the anonymous hook-and-spike clock (37), dial to the right. The original anchor escapement can be seen clearly. Much of this clock is iron; though the wheels of course are in brass. The hoop and spurs can be seen quite well. There is no backplate but a back strap to which the alarm work is attached. The double-headed alarm hammer runs up through guiding lugs on this back strap into the inside of the bell. The bell attaches by a normal, though sturdy, iron bell stand. The wheel arbors have no taper, but have interesting early wheel collets.

39. View looking down on to the top plate of the anonymous hook-and-spike wall clock of about 1710-20 (37), the bell removed for this purpose. The shaped hook and spurs can be seen, as can the back cock and mounting supports for the anchor escape arbor, and the double-headed alarm hammer. A circular hole at each side near the back of the clock (top of the photograph) shows where the side door pins once fitted, these doors are now missing. There are two irregular-shaped, rectangular holes in the top plate (and the bottom plate too), the purpose of which is unknown. This kind of work is sometimes known as 'clocksmith' work, being one step on from blacksmithing.

40. Ten-inch (25.5 cms) dial of a hook-and-spike wall clock by William Humphries of Southam, Warwickshire, dating from perhaps 1720-30. The clock as seen in this picture, could easily be a longcase example, though in fact it is not. The Tudor Rose and tulips theme continued in use for many years. Stylistic features on such simple clocks give little in the way of dating clues. The steel hand is original. The spandrel pattern is an unusual form of small cherub-head, used only on tiny dials such as this as the curve of its spread would not match a broad chapter ring. Filing marks can be seen on the dial-sheet, which is very thin, a feature of many such clocks.

41. Movement of the hook-and-spike wall clock by William Humphries of Southam (40). Such a clock did everything a thirty-hour longcase would do, but without the expense (and space) required by a case. The hoop and spurs can be seen to be integral in the construction. This, like most, has anchor escapement and long pendulum. Most had no backplate or side doors, and so were open to household dust. Some examples were actually housed in a wooden longcase within a few years of their making, perhaps when the owner decided the household budget would run to the extra cost. When cased they would hang from a hook in the backboard instead of having the normal seatboard arrangement.

42. Nine-inch (23 cms) square dial of a hook-and-spike wall clock made by Walter Archer of Stow-on-the-Wold in about 1720. The foliate cross centre engraving is a feature very often used by this maker. The half-hour markers of fleur-de-lis type have a dot to the centre of each circle, and this too is a very distinctive trait of this maker. The heavy single hand (of steel) is original. Note the inside hammer to the bell, similar in principle to that of a lantern clock. (Thirty-hour longcases normally have outside hammers). The absence of any corner spandrels is an unusual feature of this clock, and is not typical of other clocks by this maker or of hook-and-spike clocks in general.

43. Movement of the thirty-hour hook-and-spike wall clock by Walter Archer dating from about 1720 (42). The hoop and spurs can be seen clearly as can the inside hammer. The four upright corner posts are of iron, though on some clocks they are of brass. The movement is exactly the same in principle as a posted-movement thirty-hour longcase, sometimes called a birdcage movement. This particular clock has a tic-tac escapement, which is a variation of the anchor escapement found in almost all posted-movement clocks. The tic-tac has a very short 'anchor' covering usually only three teeth of the escape wheel. This type of clock represents a sort of half-way house between the lantern and the true thirty-hour longcase clock.

44. Dial of a ten-inch (25 cms) hook-and-spike clock of a distinctive pattern, the concentric rings decorated with wriggle engraving being known as a zigzag dial. This style was practised by a small group of Quaker clockmakers in north Oxfordshire, some of whom signed their clocks, and some of whom, as here, did not. The blued steel hand is original. The spandrel pattern of a small vase is a feature of about 1730-40. The chapter ring is skilfully engraved, but the point about the zigzag dial centre is that it could be done by a maker who did not possess engraving skills as it involved the use of an engraving tool in a guider.

45. Movement of the zigzag-dial hook-and-spike clock (44), built with original anchor escapement. The clock dates between 1730 and 1740. This is really nothing other than a thirty-hour posted-movement longcase clock, except that the integral hoop and spurs enabled it to be used as a hanging wall clock if required. What this meant in practice was that an owner could buy such a clock for wall use initially, and house it in a case later, as and when he could afford the extra cost of the case. This is exactly what happened in this instance, as the next illustration shows.

46. Very simple oak case housing the Quaker clock with the zigzag dial (44) and dating from the 1730s. The case is contemporary with the clock, but was probably bought a year or two after the clock, which hangs from the backboard of the case by a hook, exactly as if it hung on a wall fastening, instead of having the normal seatboard arrangement. By no means all hook-and-spike clocks were encased in this way, but it is a combination met with occasionally, particularly in north Oxfordshire. The case stands about 6 ft high (183 cms). The plinth is missing. Such simple cases often had no hood pillars. Turnbuckle door fastening is normal for most thirty-hour clocks.

47. Nine-inch dial (23 cms) of a clock signed 'John Sanderson of Wigton Fecit', an exceptionally interesting maker. This is one of his earliest clocks dating from the 1690s. The absence of corner spandrels and the use of admonitory verses were features used by some Quaker clockmakers in this area, and Sanderson was a Quaker for part of his life at least. The centre verse runs: 'Remember man that die thou must, And after that to judgment just' – a favourite verse of his. 'Memento Mori' is engraved in the top corners – 'Bear death in mind'. The calibration of this dial is extraordinary, each hour being divided into eight units, so that the single hand registers half-quarter units of an hour. A half-quarter of an hour was the smallest unit of time used before minutes became commonplace on clocks, which was quite late in certain regions such as Cumberland. This maker was a law to himself, and no dials of this eccentric calibration appear known by other makers. Meeting arrowheads as indication points indicate the end of the century in styling.

48. Movement of a thirty-hour posted-frame clock by John Sanderson of Wigton dating from about 1700 (not the clock in plate 47, but a very similar one by this extraordinary maker). The clock has original anchor escapement and long pendulum. It is thought that these clocks, made by a small group of clockmakers at Wigton and nearby, were an intermediate form using lantern-clock construction (feet, for example, though not finials, frets or side doors), but that they were originally mounted on wall brackets, as none have hoop or spurs. This type of clock was not made in general in the north-west, but only by a small group of isolated clockmakers at Wigton, all connected with John Sanderson who appears to have started the clockmaking trade there. Many of these clocks were later, often much later, housed in long cases. They represent an interesting half-way stage between lantern clocks and longcases, just as hook-and-spike clocks do as made by the north Oxfordshire Quakers. Longcase clocks had long been made in some regions by this time, but in Cumberland they were only just beginning. So whilst this type of clock pre-dates longcases in this area, the same does not apply nationally.

49. Eight-inch (20 cms) dial from a posted-movement clock of about 1690-1700. This is unsigned and the absence of spandrels is a feature used by some Quakers together with the lack of signature. This may indicate that this clock was Quaker-made. The fine steel hand is original. The circular ring grain can be seen in the dial-centre matting work, simply an indication of the way this maker produced his matting. The engraving is strong and bold, using an extended fleur-de-lis as a half-hour marker. Notice the fault in the chapter ring below XII, a blow-hole flaw from the casting. The chapter ring can be seen to be riveted to the dial-sheet at III and IX. The dial is here seen in dirty condition. From the dial alone it cannot be ascertained whether this is a longcase clock, a square-dial lantern clock, a hook-and-spike wall clock or a hooded clock. In fact it is a longcase.

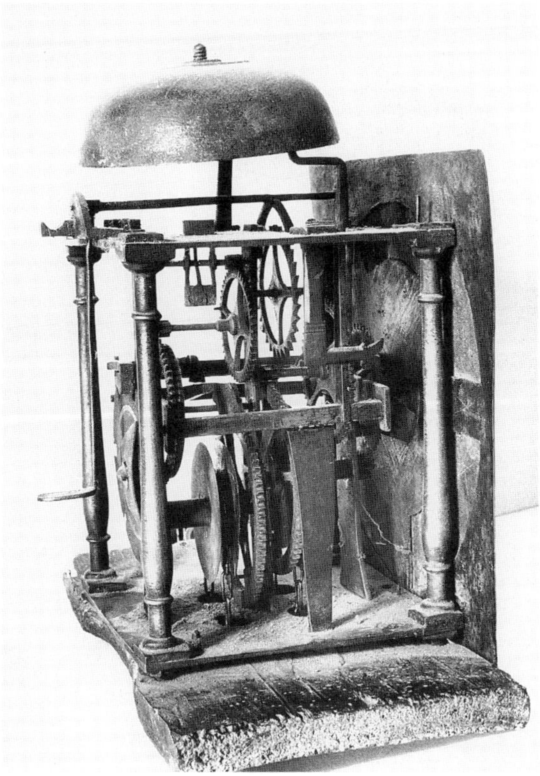

50. Movement of the anonymous 8-inch (20 cms) longcase clock (49), seen here in dirty condition, and dating from about 1690-1700. It was built with anchor escapement and long pendulum. The construction is the same as that of a contemporary lantern clock, but this never had feet, finials, frets or side doors. It is attached to its original and rather woodwormed seatboard of pine. The clock is thick with dust and is badly in need of a clean. It is possible that some makers used this basic movement construction, which they might complete in whatever form was wanted by the customer – lantern, longcase, hook-and-spike, or hooded clock. Such clocks are usually of a primitive nature, the work of isolated rural makers, though made with considerable skill; such makers are often referred to as clocksmiths.

51. Original case in pine of the unsigned clock (49). The case is crude in the extreme, was almost certainly painted originally, but was later stripped to bare pine, as is the present-day fashion. Pine is very prone to woodworm attack and it is usually only the paint which has preserved these cases to what is, for pine, a very great age. This is a very simple box designed to keep the movement dust-free and hold the weight the required distance from the floor. The long thin trunk with a narrow door, and the pillar-less hood are features of this period, as is the simple half-round D-mould on the door. The wrought-iron blacksmith-made butterfly hinges show well. Such clocks are rare survivors, since many were scrapped because of their crude nature and poor condition. They are highly important in the history of country clockmaking, but only the dedicated are enthusiastic enough to collect them today.

52. A hooded wall clock dial 7¼ ins square (18 cms) by Jones of Abingdon, date about 1710-20. The bell is removed and the bell stand can be seen at the top with the double-headed alarm hammer showing. Pictured here in unrestored condition. The 6½ inch-diameter chapter ring (16 cms) has an unusual pattern of half-hour markers, which in fact is identical with that used by Walter Archer for his lantern clocks (see plate 35). In fact this *is* a lantern-clock chapter ring. The strange corner 'spandrels' are lantern-clock dolphin-pattern blank frets, which have been cut to fit the corners. It is almost certain that Walter Archer engraved this chapter ring for a lantern clock (unless of course Jones was the one who supplied Archer with engraved work). The single hand, here marked with rust, is original. The alarm disc, with Tudor Rose motif to the centre, is original – note the tvpical lettering style of the period for the numbers, especially VII and VIII. The hood of this clock has not survived. It has an anchor escapement and long pendulum.

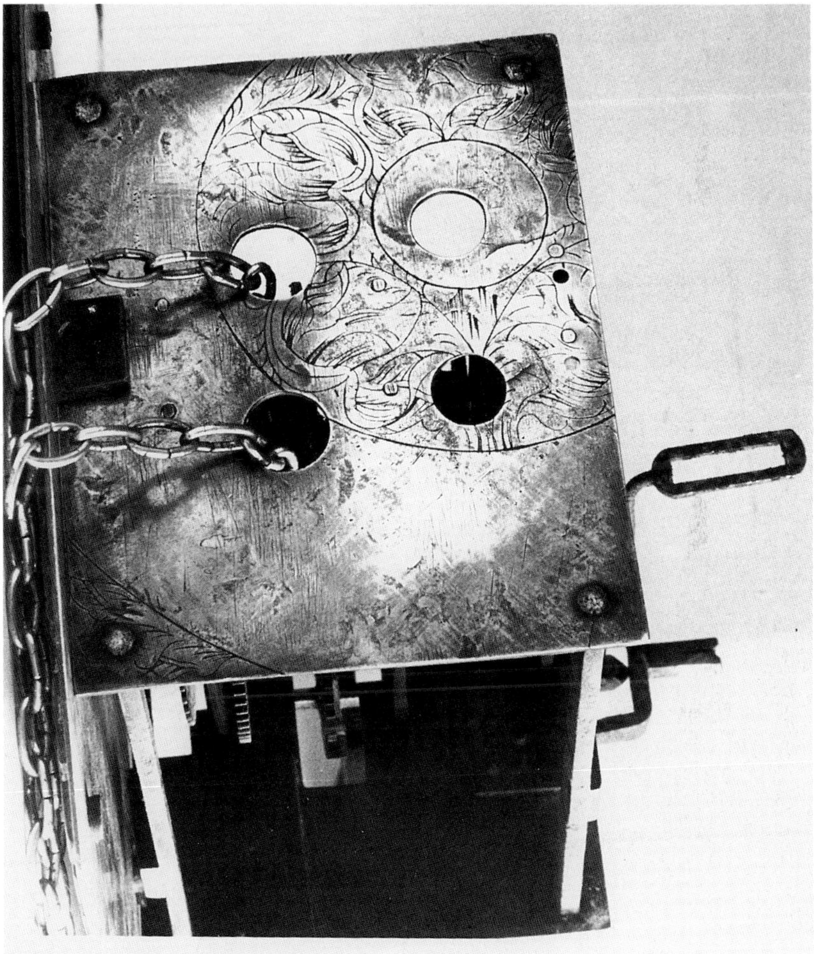

53. Movement of the Jones of Abingdon hooded clock (52) seen from below, the dial to the left. The four posts are of iron. The brass bottom plate can be seen to be part of a dial-sheet for a lantern clock. The engraved pattern is identical to that on the Archer lantern clock in plate 35. The two empty holes are for the alarm chain (here missing), but the upper one is cut off-centre to what would have been intended for the lantern dial centre, and thus it can be seen that this lantern dial-sheet was never used for a lantern clock. It was not a case of re-using an old lantern dial but of putting a sheet intended for a lantern clock to this use instead. Possibly there was some error in the engraving or some fault in the brass in the part which has been cut away, for to use it in this way meant that the time and effort spent in engraving it was wasted. The circle marks the intended dial centre, the blank zone being where the chapter ring would be overlaid. This amazing coincidence shows just how very close the connection was between lantern and hooded clocks.

54. Six-inch dial (15 cms) of an unsigned hooded wall clock, seen out of its case. The chapter ring has a diameter of 5 ins (13 cms), the alarm disc 2 ins (6 cms). The date is about 1730, the unusual mask head spandrels being from that period. The steel hand is original, the bluing polished away. The half-hour marker is a diamond shape (sometimes called a lozenge shape) and was a feature sometimes used by Quaker clockmakers at this time. Some Quakers felt they should not sign their work as that would be a sign of vanity. So this clock might be unsigned because it was made by a strict Quaker clockmaker – or it might not be, as by no means all unsigned clocks were Quaker-made. The numbering on the alarm disc can be seen to be distinctly later in style than that on the clock by Jones (plate 52). The movement is a plated one with anchor escapement. The hood has not survived.

55. Typical early eighteenth century hooded clock, unsigned as many were. The hood is of pine, here painted to simulate a more highly-figured and expensive wood. This is a single-hander, as most are, with its original hand of blued steel. The dial is about 6 ins square (15 cms). Note the alarm disc in the centre, here with the VII numeral set to the hour hand 'tail', being the time the alarm will next release. The simple half-hour markers are in the form of a fleur-de-lis. Quarter-hour units are marked along the inner edge of the chapter ring. Such clocks were normally non-striking (timepieces), because of their anticipated use in or close to a bedroom. Anchor escapement and long pendulum, the latter removed in the photograph. Non-striking clocks, as here, will often run on quite a small weight of around 4 lbs (1.8 kg); a striking clock requires more power with a weight of about twice that size. It is very hard to ascribe a region of origin to such unsigned clocks, but this was not a popular type of clock in the north and most come from southern central England.

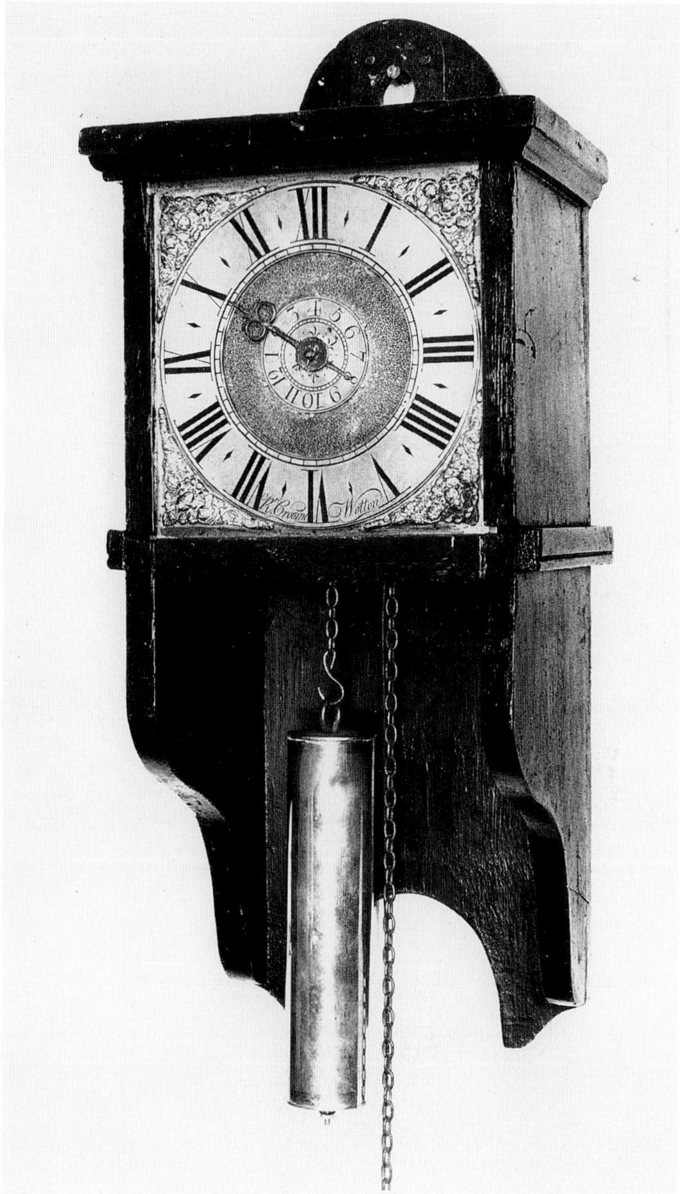

56. Hooded clock dating from about 1765 by Robert Croome of Wotton-under-Edge, Gloucestershire. The hood is of pine, painted green. The dial is about 6 ins (15 cms) square. The spandrels are of a late form and poorly cast, but this impression is made worse because they are clogged with dried metal polish. This is a timepiece with alarm work, as most hooded clocks were, striking not being desired in a clock which would be hung within earshot of the bedroom. The steel hand is original. These later examples often have a matted dial centre, in the same way that a longcase dial of this period would. The clock has a posted movement, anchor escapement and long pendulum. In the photograph the going weight is visible, but the alarm chain and weight are missing. This particular hood is an unusual construction in that there is no glass and the hood top slides down on to the shelf section, a groove in the top part sliding on to the dial edge as a restraint. Most hooded clocks have a hood which slides forward just like a longcase hood.

57. Anonymous hooded clock, an alarm timepiece (i.e. non-striking), with circular single-sheet brass dial of 6 inch diameter (15 cms) and dating from about 1760-70. The plated movement has anchor escapement and pendulum of the long type but is only half the usual length. The hand, of blued steel, appears to be original. The larger weight is to drive the going train, the smaller one for the alarm wind. The hood is of oak and unusually shaped, based on the circular dial. These simple cottage alarm-clocks were made for cheapness and robustness, and unsigned examples such as this one are not easy to date accurately.

58. Silvered single-sheet dial of a hooded clock by Charles Raymond of Lydeway, Wiltshire, dating from about 1770-80. This is a very handsome dial for that type, about 6 ins square (15 cms). It has a plated movement, anchor escapement and long pendulum. The blued steel hand is original and of an interesting pattern. The single-sheet dial fashion in these small clocks falls mostly into the 1770-1800 period. Some can be totally lacking in decoration, but this clock is charmingly engraved with all manner of floral sprays. The alarm disc is original – note how well the hand boss fits into the engraved pattern in the disc centre, and how the disc itself stands against an engraved background of dots on the main dial-sheet. The bell stands proud on its stand, the second steel rod within the bell being the shaft of the alarm hammer. Alarm hammers almost always fit within the bell, as here. The hood is not pictured.

59. Hooded clock in walnut, a most unusual wood for these cheaper cottage type of clocks. The silvered single-sheet dial is 6 ins wide, 8 ins high (15 cms by 20 cms). Here there is nothing in the way of decoration, the only engraving on the dial being informative in the shape of the numbers and the name circle, T. Smith of Edgeware. The date is a little difficult to pin down with these plain dials, but about 1780 to 1790 would seem to fit. The blued steel hand is original. The hood of the clock slides forward for access, like that of a longcase clock. The alarm disc can be seen in the dial centre and the second rope, on the right, is for the alarm weight, which is removed in the photograph. The backboard of the hood has some interesting shaping to it, and altogether this is a well-designed and well-thought-out hood from a stylistic point of view. The backboard itself is oak, the rest solid walnut. The movement is of the plated type.

60. Single-sheet silvered dial of a most unusual hooded clock being a key-wound eight-day example. The dial measures 6½ ins high by 4½ ins wide (16 cms by 11 cms), the maker is Sterling of Dublin, and the date about 1790. Unlike most hooded clocks this is a two-hander and, also unlike most, this is obviously a more costly 'gentleman's' version. The second winding-square is for the alarm wind. On alarm clocks the alarm time is set by rotating the disc till the required call time number registers on the tail of the (hour) hand; as set here this clock would ring off at just after eight. The hands are of blued steel and are original. Decoration is limited on this dial because of its small size.

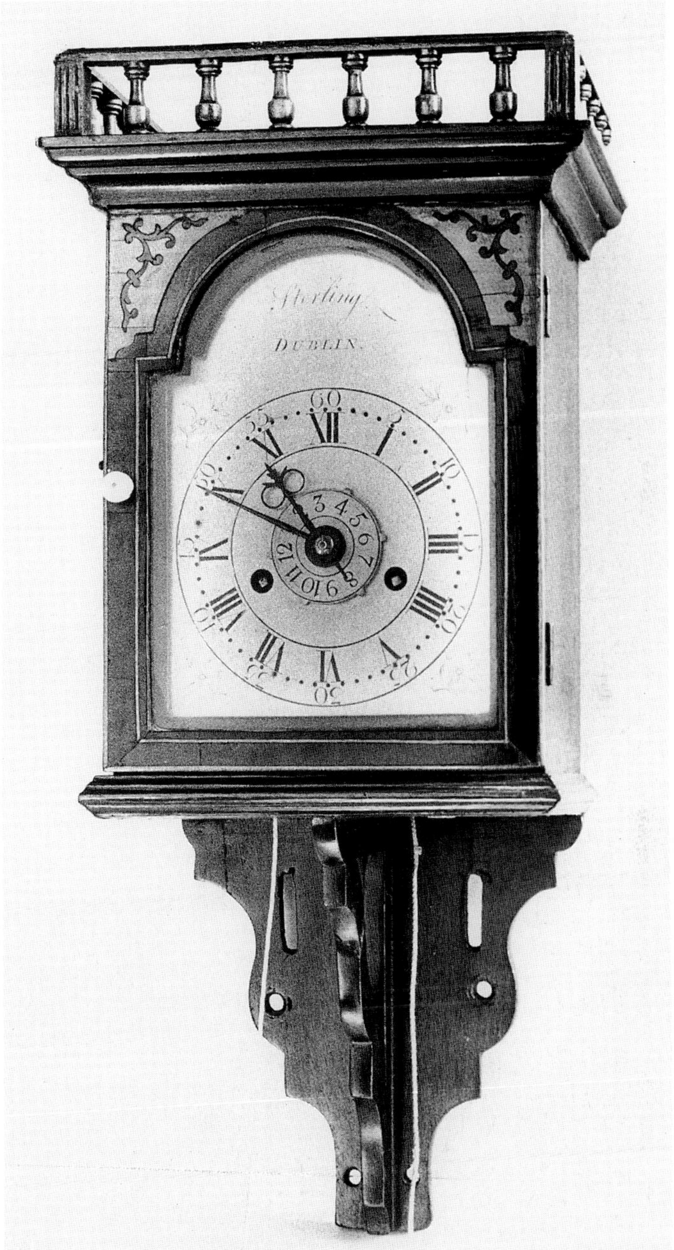

61. Case of the hooded clock by Sterling of Dublin (60), made in mahogany with fancy-wood inlay above the arch and a most unusual gallery around the top. The total height is about 16 ins (42 cms), width 7½ ins (19 cms). The style is clearly far more sophisticated than the average cottage hooded clock, perhaps made for the landing of a grander house. The clock has a verge escapement and a short pendulum, which is concealed within the hood. This was probably for neatness in avoiding a pendulum projecting below, something not considered important for a cottage version.

2 *Longcase clocks*

THIRTY-HOUR BRASS DIALS AND EIGHT-DAY BRASS DIALS

The introduction of the pendulum to England by Ahasuerus Fromanteel in 1658 made the longcase clock possible. From the very first it was available in thirty-hour form or in eight-day duration, as well as in examples running for three months, six months and even a year, though these long-duration clocks were always uncommon. The passage of time has meant that today any longcase clock made before the 1680s is a very uncommon item. The earliest clocks are likely to have been made in London, since in some provincial areas local clockmaking had barely begun by 1700.

As the lantern clock became increasingly obsolete, some forms of thirty-hour longcase clock can be seen to spring from the lantern form, as the lantern and variants of it became encased for protection, and varying shapes of dial were adopted. Ultimately, the lantern clock died out except in the form of small travelling alarm-clocks, which were conveniently portable, especially if they retained the verge escapement and short pendulum.

However, there were thirty-hour longcase clocks from the first years of the pendulum (immediately post-1658), long before the decline of the lantern clock. Thirty-hour longcase clocks were made in both plated and posted form from the very beginning, and it is unlikely that either version preceded the other. The choice as to posted or plate-framed movement was probably mostly one of individual preference on the part of the maker, and is not necessarily an indication of greater age. It is true generally that the posted movement thirty-hour longcase was principally, though not exclusively, a product of the south of England where the lantern clock tradition remained strongest. It may be that this southern bias arose because of the lantern-clock making tradition there with which southern makers would always have been familiar.

By the middle of the eighteenth century, the posted-movement longcase was rapidly falling out of fashion in favour of the plated one. From the late eighteenth century onwards, these by now old-fashioned clocks were mostly restricted to rural areas, where tradition died hardest – in East Anglia, for example, posted movements lasted even into the nineteenth century.

The thirty-hour clock was available from the very first with one or two hands, and it is not correct, as is sometimes imagined, to assume that a single-hander is necessarily older than a two-hander. The single-hand version was essentially made for those who were less familiar with the household clock, and found it easier to read what was in many ways an indoor sundial. Two hands were found to be confusing enough for some customers to insist on the older system of single-hand time reading on their thirty-hour clocks even as late as the end of the eighteenth century. The single-handed clock was virtually always a thirty-hour clock (though some were later 'converted' to eight-day duration by replacing the movement). A few, a very few, single-handed clocks were made with eight-day duration, again probably for owners who wanted the eight-day convenience, but the traditional single-hand time reading. Eight-day single-handed clocks are so uncommon that a search of all the published books on clocks is unlikely to reveal more than half a dozen examples.

The thirty-hour longcase clock existed alongside the eight-day version as a cheaper alternative. It was more often purchased for cottage or farmhouse use. It had fewer working parts, was generally less sensitive to uneven levels, and was more capable of being wound and cared for by the owner. In rural areas, the thirty-hour was *the* widespread type of clock. In the towns, the clockmaker would often include weekly winding of an eight-day clock as a part of his service, and his presence was conveniently close in case of any problem.

The thirty-hour was therefore almost always a cottage type of clock, its lower height requirement for its weight-drop enabling a smaller clock to be made which suited cottage ceilings. Most thirty-hour clocks had countwheel striking (outside the backplate). A few had rack striking, notably if they were made that way to offer a repeating facility. With eight-day clocks, the presence of outside countwheel striking is an early feature, discontinued in favour of other principles by about 1700. But thirty-hour clocks retained outside countwheel strike until they ceased to be made, which was well into the second quarter of the nineteenth century.

Most thirty-hour clocks have three wheels in the going train, and hence they do not have a seconds dial, since the wheel behind the seconds dial position turns anti-clockwise. Just a few clocks, mostly Victorian, did have anti-clockwise rotating seconds hands, running from the normal three-wheel train, but this was considered by most to be unprofessional and was seldom used. Some thirty-hour clocks have a four-wheel train, and these may well have a normal seconds hand rotating clockwise. The four-wheel train versions are usually well-made clocks, and avoid some of the slop in the hands of a three-wheel thirty-hour.

In London, the majority of clocks made were of eight-day duration; in fact, thirty-hour clocks made there (as longcases) are most unusual. In many provincial areas it was not until about 1700 that clockmaking got under way at all; with the exception of certain large provincial cities which had clockmakers within twenty years of London. It must have been an exceptionally difficult task for the first clockmakers to convince their potential customers, who had always lived without clocks, that they now ought to have one. Life on the land was determined by hours of light or darkness, not clock time. Since such people often begrudged spending money on a clock, they would usually opt for the cheaper versions. This is why the great majority of the earlier clocks in provincial clockmaking tend to be thirty-hour examples. In many of the more far-flung provinces an eight-day clock dating from before 1720 is an unusual item; and in rural areas, the thirty-hour clock always remained the more widespread type until the end of native clockmaking.

The older clocks tend to have smaller dials than later ones. In thirty-hour clocks some were made with 9-inch dials, but 10 inches is more normal. Those provincial areas starting late in clocks would tend to come into the size group relative to their starting date, so, for example, 11 inches is the smallest size usually met with in most northern counties. In the north, and especially the north-west, there always seems to have been a fondness for large dials, and a north-western clock will often have a dial an inch or two larger in size than a contemporary clock from the south. This trend continued well into white-dial times.

Eight-day dials developed from the square into the arched style by about 1700, though the square dial continued to be used, especially for clocks where height was limited. Thirty-hour clocks were slower to take on the arched trend, probably once more because their primary requirement was small height. Few thirty-hour clocks will be found with an arched dial before about 1750, and arched dials were always in the minority in brass-dial thirty-hour clocks.

Thirty-hour clocks were wound by a continuous chain or rope

inside the case, which operated both going and striking train on a single weight. There is no evidence that either rope or chain pre-dates the other. Chain was more costly, because more work was involved in its making, and a chain-driven thirty-hour clock worked out about 1s.6d. more than one with rope.

When new a thirty-hour brass-dial clock would have cost about £3.10s.0d. in the mid-eighteenth century. The case was extra, a simple pine case costing ten shillings, a simple oak one £1.

A new eight-day clock with its dial would have cost from £4.10s.0d. to £5, plus the case cost. A good mahogany case could easily cost £10, ten times as much as a simple oak one. Clocks with special features, such as three-train musical clocks, would have been considerably more expensive, as were clocks of any kind when made by famous London clockmakers.

WHITE DIALS

A new kind of clock dial was introduced in about 1770, principally for longcase clocks, but also for bracket clocks and wall clocks. This was a japanned dial, at the time referred to as a white dial, though today the term painted dial is often used. These were made by specialist japanners, most of whom were in Birmingham, and the clockmaker could not make these dials himself, but had to purchase them either through a wholesaler or direct from the dial-makers. This kind of dial was made until the end of native longcase clockmaking in about 1870.

White dials were first advertised by Messrs Osborne and Wilson of Birmingham in 1772, though the occurrence of occasional examples of a partly experimental nature suggests that there may have been earlier dialmakers whose names are not known to us. Many white dials have the dial-maker's name on the back.

Many early white dials were supplied complete with an iron backing plate, known as a falseplate, the purpose of which was to help the clockmaker attach his movement and avoid the problem whereby a pre-fixed dial foot might meet up with the movement awkwardly, e.g. where a movement pillar would foul against it. Falseplates were often impressed with the dial-maker's name. Where the name of the dial-maker can be established, this forms a very useful secondary means of identification and dating, as the names and working dates of most dial-makers are recorded.

White dials rapidly gained favour with the public and, almost from the point of their introduction, the brass dial began to fall from popularity. By about 1790, most longcase clocks had the newer kind of white dial, and the brass dial was virtually obsolete by 1800, except for a few regions such as the West Country, where tradition lingered longer. In London too, the brass dial was often retained late, as it was in parts of Scotland. It was often kept for use on such items as regulators.

As a result of the centralization of much of the white dial-making business, the styles follow a progressive sequence and are easily understood and easily dated. White-dial styles break down conveniently into three phases of style. Period One runs from the beginning (say 1770) to 1800. Period Two runs from 1800 to 1830. Period Three runs from 1830 to 1870. Within each period there are usually several factors which enable a dial to be placed within its group with some certainty. The numbering pattern is the most consistent of these features, but there are others which are explained in the captions.

The dials of bracket clocks and certain kind of wall clock also followed this trend, and can often be placed in period as easily as longcase clocks can.

The hands of clocks also followed a regular pattern change over the years, and original hands can often be a useful aid to dating.

Case styles developed too. However, case styles also varied from region to region, and the whole subject of cases is a highly complicated one, far more complicated than the trends in dial styles.

Obviously not every dial met with will fall strictly within the guidelines indicated. In particular, the exact dates suggested for the limit of each period style may have to be regarded as slightly flexible. But the principles do hold true.

One aspect to beware of is a dial which has been 'restored' in the sense of re-painted. Today white dials are usually restored with great care to preserve the style of the original. In the past this was not always the case, and it is sometimes possible to come across a dial where the style of numbers clashes totally with the style of corner decoration simply because the numbers have been re-painted incorrectly. Numbers re-painted in this way are usually obvious from close examination, though perhaps not from a photograph.

62. Nine-inch-square (23 cms) brass dial from a very early thirty-hour longcase clock made by John Williamson of Temple Bar, London. This maker moved to London in December 1682 and had removed to Leeds by December 1683. The seconds hand is missing in the photograph and the main hands are replacements. The dial engraving is of outstanding quality. The signing of a clock dial on a drapery swag, as here, was a short-lived fashion of this period. The clock is a short-duration pull-wind example running for three days on a four pound weight (1.8 kg). It further chimes the quarter-hours on four bells at each of the three quarters, striking the hour count on the hour, all by means of a single external countwheel and all running from the one strike train. The tiny cherub-head spandrels are found only on very small dials at this time. At this early date minutes are engraved *inside* the minute band, and seconds dials are usually numbered every fifth unit, as here. Pull-wind clocks of London make are very uncommon and very rarely of this exceptional quality and innovation.

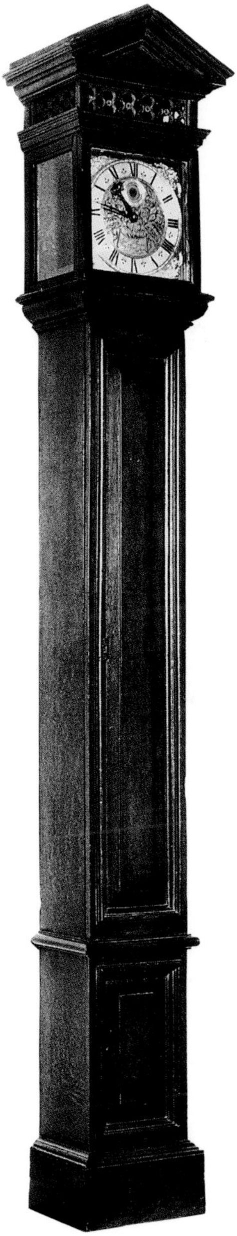

63. Oak case housing the John Williamson clock (62). The architectural style, the very slender body with no waist, and the long door fitting flush over the case side-pieces, are all features indicative of this very early period (*c*. 1680), as are the very large side windows to the hood. The case originally had bun feet, now missing. These cases are sometimes described as 'coffin clocks', since they did not have a wider base section as was the norm later on. The base is simply a continuation of the sides, interrupted only by a moulding which separates the 'base' section. Height 7 ft 6 ins (229 cms). The hood was originally rising, later converted to slide forward.

64. Ten-inch (25.5 cms) dial of a thirty-hour single-handed clock by John Waklin, dating from *c.*1700. This maker's place of working is not known, but judging by the style it would be in the south-west of England. The spandrel pattern of twin cherubs holding a crown was introduced at the end of the old century and remained popular for about twenty years, and longer with some clockmakers. The dial-centre is most beautifully engraved, based on a central Tudor Rose motif and running into ornate scrollwork. The unusual hour hand of blued steel is original. The movement is of the posted type. A country clock, but of exquisite workmanship.

65. Ten-inch dial (25.5 cms) of a single-handed thirty-hour unsigned clock dating from about 1710-20. Heavy fleurs-de-lis mark the half hours, rather similar to the markings of a lantern clock. The engraved dial-centre has a pattern based largely on tulips. The spandrels of twin cherubs with crossed maces supporting a crown are a typical pattern of the day. The hand is original, of blued steel, and shows considerable styling. The clock is not signed and might well be Quaker work, as some Quakers felt it was a sign of vanity to sign their dials. The movement is of the birdcage type, and the clock is probably from the Oxfordshire area.

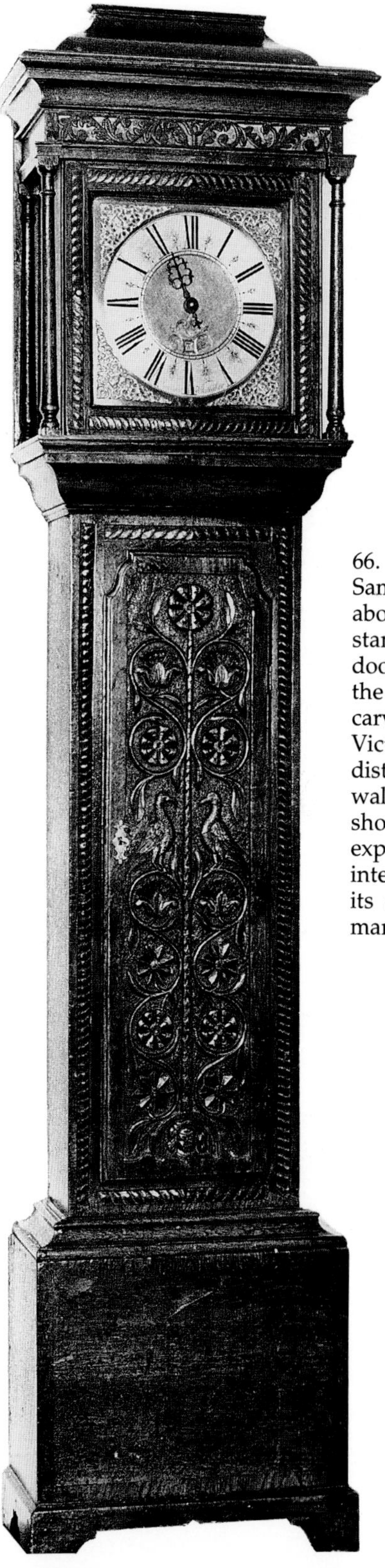

66. Oak-cased thirty-hour single-handed clock by Samuel Whittaker of Middleton (Manchester) made about 1710-20, with original hour hand. The case stands 6 ft 11 ins (211 cms) and is carved on the trunk door and hood door only. Some clocks were carved at the time of manufacture, but the great majority of carved ones were carved much later, many in Victorian times. It is difficult, if not impossible, to distinguish original carving from later. This case has walnut crossbanding around some of its sections (it shows most clearly on the base), and one would not expect crossbanding to have been applied if the intention was to carve up to, or in to, it. The hood has its original caddy top, which is good to see as so many have been removed to reduce height.

67. Ten-inch (25.5 cms) dial of a thirty-hour single-handed clock dating a little before 1720 by James Wolley (or Woolley) of Codnor in Derbyshire, a well-known clockmaker, eccentric and miser. The original hand is of steel and appears bright as the bluing has been polished away. The dial is edged in herringbone engraving, sometimes known as wheatear, a feature fashionable in the first quarter of the eighteenth century. The circular date-box was not used by every maker, but it is found normally only at this early period – square boxes were more usual. Two flower-heads are engraved on to the matted dial-centre in the position where winding-holes would appear on an eight-day clock. This was probably to break up what would otherwise be a plain dial centre and from a distance may give the superficial appearance of an eight-day clock. This practice was confined to the northern part of England and was used by many, though not all, clockmakers. The movement is of the plated type.

68. Oak case, darkened almost to black with age, housing the Wolley of Codnor clock (67) and believed original to it. Height about 6 ft 7 ins (200 cms). The bun feet and plinth are replaced and the base may have been reduced slightly in height, though some bases of rustic clocks at this time are unusually shallow. This is a simple country joiner-made case, with wrought-iron strap hinges, no pillars to the hood, and eccentrically heavy top-of-trunk moulding (the hood top mould is a replacement). The bull's-eye lenticle glass is an early feature which fell out of fashion by the 1740s; its purpose was to catch the glint of the pendulum bob as it swung. The flat-topped trunk door with half-round (D-shaped) moulding is an early feature. At each side of the trunk are bobbin-like applied turnings, hollowed out inside, to allow for a pendulum swing greater than the trunk width. These are sometimes found on early clocks with slender cases.

69. Ten-inch (25.5 cms) dial from a single-handed thirty-hour clock of 1720-30 by Robert Flower of Retford, a little-known maker. The clock was photographed in dirty condition, so that the matted centre shows up imperfectly. The spandrels are of the same pattern (twin cherubs with crown) as those on the Burton clocks (71-74), but can be seen to differ in detail. The fleur-de-lis half-hour marker is very much smaller, and the engraving style is generally more restrained than the Burton clocks, a feature indicative of the more southerly region. Meeting arrowheads are again used on the hour band. The steel hand is believed original, and has lost its bluing through polishing. The movement is of the plated type. A bird in the matted centre was a common feature on many clocks from the Midlands. This dial is more conventional than the Burton dials of similar age, and lacks their boldness and strength of character.

70. Oak case of the thirty-hour clock by Robert Flower of Retford (70), height about 6 ft 10 ins (208 cms). The case is not dissimilar in general style to the Burton case. The trunk door has an arched top, sometimes called a break-arch or broken arch, intended to indicate an arch with a step at each side. These simple overall lines formed the outline of many a cottage clock for almost a century from about 1690. The lenticle glass in the door was a feature of many clocks and lasted until about 1740 in country areas. The case has a lock and escutcheon, which is a little unusual for a thirty-hour clock since one would not expect to lock and unlock it every day at winding time. It is more usual for thirty-hour clocks to have a turnbuckle.

72. Ten-inch (25.5 cms) dial from the thirty-hour single-handed clock by William Burton of Kendal dating from the 1720s. The engraving is bold and skilfully done. This has a classic 'penny moon' feature with a silvered moon disc and silvered stars on a black-waxed background. The lunar date shows below the moon, and the calendar date in the box above VI. The hand is of blued steel and is original. The twin-cherub spandrel pattern is still in use. Meeting arrowheads are used in indicating the hour points, and are incorporated into the half-hour markers, and arrowheads are often used in the early eighteenth century. The movement is of the plated type. A fine dial by a very competent maker.

71. Oak case of a penny moon clock by William Burton of Kendal (72), standing about 6 ft 8 ins (204 cms). One reason that early clocks are more highly regarded by collectors than later ones is that the smaller dials allow the cases to be more slender and graceful. This is especially the case with early thirty-hour clocks, which have smaller dials than eight-day clocks of the same period. Early thirty-hour clocks, as neat and slender as this one are highly desirable items. The case is preserved in excellent condition and retains its original caddy top, so often removed to reduce height. The bracket foot is probably a replacement, hardly surprising with a cottage clock which has stood on damp floors for two-and-a-half centuries. Replacement feet are not regarded as any detriment by collectors.

73. Ten-inch dial (25.5 cms) from another thirty-hour clock with single hand, also by William Burton of Kendal. The number 1 is engraved on various parts inside the movement, and might have been the first clock of his making (or of his numbering, though he did not continue numbering in a sequence later). Date between 1720 and 1730. The circular face below XII appears to be a penny moon, but is in fact a fixed face with a moving panel behind it, rocking on an extension from the anchor arbor, producing a rocking-eyes effect. The calendar here is a rotating disc type (an unusual form as early as this), though here its fixed pointer is missing. The steel hour hand is original, though its bluing has been polished away leaving it as bright steel, which of course was never the original treatment. The dial is pictured in uncleaned state. The matting to the centre is performed deliberately in circles, whereas some makers worked this in random and some in vertical grain – all a matter of individual taste and the whim of the maker.

74. Detail of the hood of the rocking-eyes clock by William Burton of Kendal (73) dating from the 1720s, the dial now cleaned and the hand blued. The case is of oak and it can be seen to have retained its original patina from generations of waxing by proud owners. The wood has taken on a hard, steely appearance and is cold to the touch. This is obviously a country case, sometimes called a farmhouse case, yet it is well made and with considerable skill and knowledge of contemporary case styling. Dowel pegs can be seen holding the joints in places, e.g. the top right-hand corner of the hood door shows up well. The shaping to the trunk door top is characteristic of several shapes of similar nature on northern clocks of this time, whereas southern cases more usually had flat-topped trunk doors.

75. Eleven-inch (28 cms) dial of a thirty-hour single-handed longcase clock by Joshua Mos(e)ley of Penistone, Yorkshire, dating from the 1730s or early 1740s. The blued steel hand is original – in fact the hands of single-handed clocks were usually very sturdy and have a high survival rate compared to the flimsier hands of two-handed clocks. The penny moon has the lunar date on its outer rim and shows through a curved slot in the dial. The calendar also shows through a curved mouth. Note the rivets showing on the chapter ring at XII and VI, on its inner edge. These hold the chapter ring to the dial, and a riveted ring is a sign of rustic work. The snag with rivets is that they have to be broken off so that the dial can be cleaned professionally, and replaced by new ones. A better system, and one used more often on eight-day clocks, was to attach the chapter ring by means of short 'feet', which pinned behind the dial. This is a handsome dial of considerable character.

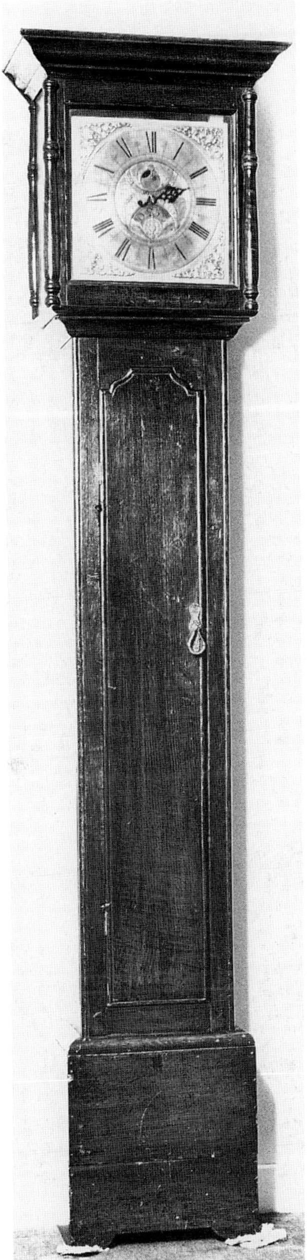

76. The movement of the Joshua Mos(e)ley clock (75) is of plated construction. It has 'stepped' plates, i.e. is cut away at the base of the plates, which was done essentially to save brass, though it was also used for decorative effect. The top two movement pillars are of brass with turned centre knops, as normal. However, the lower two are of square-section iron rod, cheaper but equally effective, and this was a system used by a few rural makers. The dial pillar on the lower right can also be seen to be square-section rod. The tapered bellstand is a notable, early feature, as later ones are of uniform thickness. The two discs can be seen plainly behind the dial, being the moon disc and calendar disc. Each is knocked on twice a day by half a point by means of a wedge on the hour pipe, a simple system that requires no additional gearing for drive.

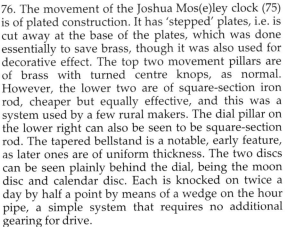

77. Simple and unusually slim oak case of the Mos(e)ley clock (75). The hood pillars are turned in an interesting manner and are attached to the hood door – three-quarter pillars at the front and half pillars at the back, a feature found more often in the south than the north. The door is a left-hand opener – it was possible to have left or right handed opening on request. The base is original, though the very small base-to-trunk moulding is unusually small and reminiscent of London clocks of many years earlier. Wide top-of-hood moulds are a feature of many cottage clocks of this age. The colour is dark, the result of years of waxing in dust and grime – Penistone was coal-mining country.

78. Ten-inch (25.5 cms) dial of a single-handed thirty-hour longcase clock dating from about 1740 by Robert Henderson of Scarborough, a Quaker. Blank corners without spandrels were a feature sometimes used by Quakers as it expressed simplicity. This dial is a little difficult to date with any certainty. The meeting arrowhead half-hour markers were often used at the beginning of the eighteenth century. The matted dial-centre is quite plain except for three decorative roundels. These are there purely to break up what would otherwise be a very bare dial-centre, but they are positioned where seconds feature and winding-holes would appear on an eight-day, though oddly enough the two lower roundels are not level with each other. The hand is of blued steel and is original. This clock has a plated movement, as was normal in the north.

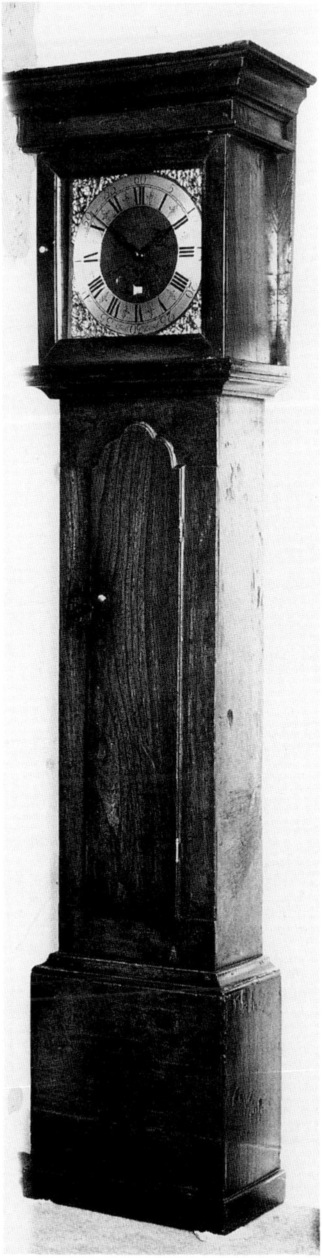

79. Eleven-inch (28 cms) dial of a two-handed thirty-hour clock by Samuel Parrat of Killington, Westmorland dating from about 1760. The matted centre can be seen to have the grain running in a circular pattern. The blued steel hands are original. Notice that the half-hour markers are still present, but the inner chapter ring band has dropped from use by this time – normally a sign that the period is into the second half of the century. The spandrels are one version of the female head, but here they appear to be poorly defined, though this is aggravated by the fact that the dial is photographed in dirty condition. Screw-fitted hands were quite often employed in the north, though pin-fitting was normal, north or south. The movement is a normal one of plated form.

80. The case of the Parrat clock (79) is a simple cottage case made of elm. The typical elm figuring can be seen most obviously in the trunk door. Elm was far more prone to woodworm than oak, and many elm cases must have perished because of worm. Many elm cases were originally painted in the same way that pine ones were, though this particular example shows no signs of that. Some simple cases, such as this one, did not have pillars to the hood. The height is about 6 ft 3 ins (190 cms).

81. Eleven-inch (28 cms) dial of a two-handed thirty-hour clock of about 1760 by William Hargraves of Settle. The absence of half-hour markers and quarter-hour divisions to the inner chapter ring edge, makes these dials look plain alongside earlier ones. The name is on a recessed plaque. The mouth type of calendar was popular on many thirty-hour dials after mid-century. The hands are of blued steel and are believed original, despite being 'over length' if we take the hour and minute rings as being a guide. The two ringed holes in the dial are imitation winding-holes (a thirty-hour clock was pull-wound and does not need them). Not only do these fill up an otherwise plain dial centre, but they might at first sight give the appearance of an eight-day (and therefore costlier) clock. This was probably designed to impress the neighbours. Dummy winding-holes were a common feature in certain parts of north-west England, but are not found in the south. Notice the chapter-ring rivets showing at III and IX on the inner edge of the ring.

82. The movement of the Hargraves clock (81) can be seen to be a musical one, having an extra train for the music. It plays a tune every fourth hour on a nest of six bells with six hammers. The second countwheel regulates the musical playing and can be seen to have three slots in a twelve-hour-rotating disc. The musical barrel with its pins for triggering the hammers can be seen clearly. This is a plated form of movement but the plates are clearly much broader than usual to accommodate the musical train. Musical thirty-hour longcase clocks are very unusual.

83. Eleven-inch (28 cms) dial from a two-handed thirty-hour clock of about 1760 by Michael Waggitt of Richmond, Yorkshire. The matting to the dial-centre is coarse-grained – each maker had his own way of doing this and some preferred a fine, some a heavier grain. The reason behind this matting was so that the hands would stand out clearly without reflections. Both hands are original, of blued steel. By this time half-hour and quarter-hour divisions have ceased to be marked. The strange dot between the 5 and 10 numerals and another between 20 and 25 at first seem very puzzling. These appear in fact to be rivets holding the chapter ring to the dial sheet – a third one can be seen at the base of the IX numeral. The mouth calendar is here shaped a little bit differently to most, but that is no more than a whim of the maker.

84. Thirty-hour single-handed longcase clock made about 1770 by Thomas Stockton of Yarm, North Yorkshire. A single-hander is unusual in the north as late as this. Obviously single-handed clocks retained at all times the quarter- and half-hour units, which by now had ceased to appear on two-handers. This kind of floral decoration to the dial-centre is of a different nature to earlier floral engraving. The pattern is centred around what appear to be two winding-holes but in fact are dummy holes, simply circles engraved on. The blued steel hand is original. Meeting arrowheads for the hour indicators are unusually late in this example. Diamond-shaped half-hour markers are also a feature found earlier, so this clock has a number of features of archaic style. The rococo spandrels, however, are typical of the 1770s.

85. Twelve-inch (30.5 cms) dial from a thirty-hour two-handed longcase clock of about 1770 by George Miles of Sodbury. This is a single-sheet brass dial, that is the type where all the details are engraved on to a single sheet of brass so that there is no separate chapter ring, etc. The wavy minute band, sometimes known as a 'Dutch' minute band, is a feature found usually only on a composite dial with separate chapter ring, and its presence on this type of dial is very unusual. Engraved scenes within the dial-centre are quite common at this period, especially in the south-west. The corner themes represent the Four Seasons, very unusual in this form of engraved corner decoration. Unlike most thirty-hour clocks, this one has a seconds dial, involving an extra wheel in the going train to reverse direction of drive. Such a clock has four wheels in the going train and a four-wheel thirty-hour is regarded as better in quality than a three-wheeler. The hands are of blued steel and are original throughout. Notice how well the seconds-hand boss fits the engraved pattern of the starburst. Seconds numbered in tens rather than fives is usually an indication of a post-1750 dial.

86. Eleven-inch (28 cms) dial of a two-handed thirty-hour longcase clock dating from 1760-70 by William Drury of Banbury. The rococo spandrels with two crossed shells in the centre are a pattern found in the 1760s and 1770s. The absence of half-hour and quarter-hour markers are an indication that the period is well into the third quarter of the century. The non-matching hands in blued steel are believed original. The scrollwork pattern of engraving to the dial centre is typical of the 1760s and 1770s. Such engraving is always on to a polished (i.e. un-matted) background. The movement is of the plated type. The engraving is well done without being in any way extraordinarily special. It is a typical thirty-hour clock of the day of respectable quality.

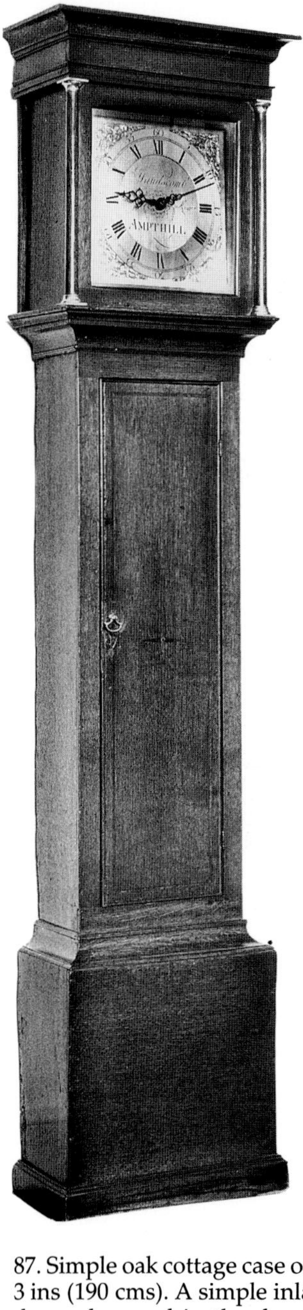

88. Eleven-inch (28 cms) dial of a two-handed thirty-hour clock of the 1770s by Ebenezer Handscomb of Ampthill, Bedfordshire. The spandrel pattern was used in the 1770s and 1780s and the restrained use of centre decorative engraving with slightly more formal flower-sprays and bold block lettering indicates that this is a late clock for a brass dial, possibly even dating from the 1780s. By this period no half-hour or quarter-hour markers appear. The non-matching hands are of blued steel, and may be original, though the hour hand is unusually large for the dial and might perhaps be a replacement (though a genuine hand of the right period). The movement is of the plated type.

87. Simple oak cottage case of the Ebenezer Handscomb clock (88) standing about 6 ft 3 ins (190 cms). A simple inlaid line of mahogany banding is set in an inch from the door edge, and in the door centre a small starburst of inlay. The door has what appears to be its original turnbuckle, in what is usually called an axe-drop, or English axe-drop, pattern. Many such cottage clocks had flat tops, as here, to keep the height down because of low ceilings, and the caddy top found often on northern clocks was far less common in the south. The oak shows little in the way of figuring, probably because it is not quarter-cut, but is straight sawn or slash-sawn, as it is sometimes called. Simple moulds are found more often in the south than the north, as is the flat door top which can make the case look broader than it actually is. The plinth looks old as it is washed paler in parts from the mopping of floors, but the grain is quite different to the rest of the case, so it may well be an old replacement. Such a simple case would have varied little twenty years either side of the suggested date.

89. Thirty-hour longcase clock by Henry Fisher of Preston dating from the 1760s or 1770s. This example has not only imitation winding-holes, but also dummy winding-squares, to give superficial resemblance to an eight-day clock. The winding-squares are screwed into the movement frontplate. The sparse foliate engraving is on to a matted ground, a practice mostly of north-western makers. Arched dials are unusual in thirty-hour brass-dial clocks (less so in painted dials), and even more unusual is a rocking figure in the arch, such as the rocking ship shown here. The foliate spandrels are typical of this period. The hands are non-matching in type and of blued steel. The hour hand could well be original but the minute hand, though of the right pattern, looks unduly heavy and may be a modern replacement. Dial size 12 ins (30.5 cms). Plated movement.

90. Eleven-inch (28 cms) dial from a thirty-hour longcase clock of the 1760s or 1770s by Thomas Lister of Halifax (junior). The half-circular moon dial (here a painted one, but some are engraved brass) was a popular feature in this area, especially with this maker. One of his characteristics was to make the hands in brass, when almost all other makers of this time used steel, and these are the original hands. Spandrels are typical of the period. The encroaching floral sprays to the centre are typical of this maker, as are the scalloped rings round the dial-centre. Rivets hold the chapter ring at III and IX, where the numbers are actually engraved with a kink to miss the rivet point – a typical Lister feature. An interesting maker with a very personalized style. Plated movement.

91. Carved oak case, stained near to black, of a thirty-hour longcase clock by Thomas Lister junior dating from the 1760s. This is not the clock pictured in plate 90, but a similar one by him. Carved cases are difficult to comment on with any certainty. Most are original to the clock, but were carved at a much later date. However with some makers, such as Thomas Lister, a high proportion of his cases are carved ones, which is difficult to explain if the carving was done later. Most carved ones are stained in this very dark colour, and on most examples the carving is limited to the front of the clock, the sides being plain, as here. A swan-neck pediment on a square-dial clock was more popular in some areas than others, and is frequently found in clocks from the Lancashire/ Yorkshire Pennines. Some, like this one, have a 'box top' protruding each side of the swan necks, intended as a base for finials. These finials are of wood, gessoed and gilded. These are of the flame (or flambeau) pattern, meant to represent a burning torch. The case stands about 7 ft (213 cms) and is original to the clock – but is the carving original? Dial size 11 ins (28 cms). Lister is a maker much respected in his own area.

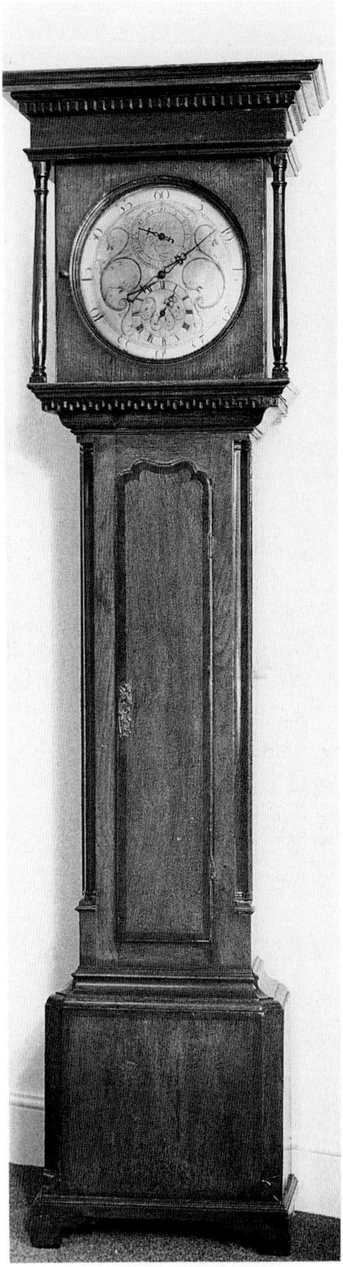

93. A very unusual round-dial thirty-hour clock with one-piece (sometimes known as a single-sheet) silvered brass dial. This dates from the 1770s, or a little either side of that decade, and what is unusual about it is that this is a regulator, usually made by a clockmaker for his own use as a master clock; its purpose was for testing the timekeeping of his other clocks. Seconds, hours and minutes all register by separate sub-dials, as was normal layout for a regulator. The minute hand (counterbalanced to reduce drag) and hour hand are of steel and are original – the bluing has been polished away so that here they appear as bright steel. The seconds hand is probably a later replacement, though it fits well for size. The scroll engraving is exceptionally fine, as one would expect if the clockmaker were making a clock for his own use. Eight-day regulators usually have some kind of maintaining power to keep the clock driving during winding. However the beauty of a thirty-hour regulator is that the pull-wind system is always in drive, even during winding. Daily winding was no problem for a clockmaker working in his own home, as this maker, Emanuel Burton of Kendal, probably did. Dial diameter 12 ins (30.5 cms). Plated movement.

92. Oak case, trimmed with mahogany crossbanding, of the regulator by Emanuel Burton of Kendal (93). The case stands about 7 ft (213 cms), and is of slender and handsome proportions, with dentil moulding below the hood topmould, and key-pattern moulding on the top-of-trunk moulding. The hood pillars are slim and swell in a graceful manner. Notice the complicated moulding between trunk and base, a shape of mould confined largely to the north-west, and very different from a much simpler, southern moulding. The base has canted corners, and so has the below-trunk moulding. Quarter pillars (strictly speaking they should be called pilasters) to the trunk help give an impression of greater slimness. The wavy doortop shape is a characteristic of many northern clocks. This is a very rare and highly collectable item. Regrettably this clock is now in the United States, as when I sold this clock some years ago, I could not find a museum here to buy it.

94. Thirteen-inch (33 cms) arched-dial longcase with rocking ship in the arch, made about 1780 by Lot Barwise of Cockermouth. This is a thirty-hour clock with dummy winding-holes to give eight-day appearance. The case is typical in style of a mahogany or perhaps an oak case of the day, but is made in pine, ebonized to a black finish. Pine cases were normally of simpler, cottage style, and this is an unusually grand style for a pine clock. It is also unusual for ebonizing to occur as late as this, as most pine clocks of this period would have been painted. This is altogether a most unusual item, presumably made specifically to order on the wishes of a particular customer. The hands (difficult to see in the photograph) are later replacements from a Victorian painted dial clock. A very interesting clock, though not to everyone's taste. Height about 7 ft 8 ins (234 cms). The brass eagle finial is original.

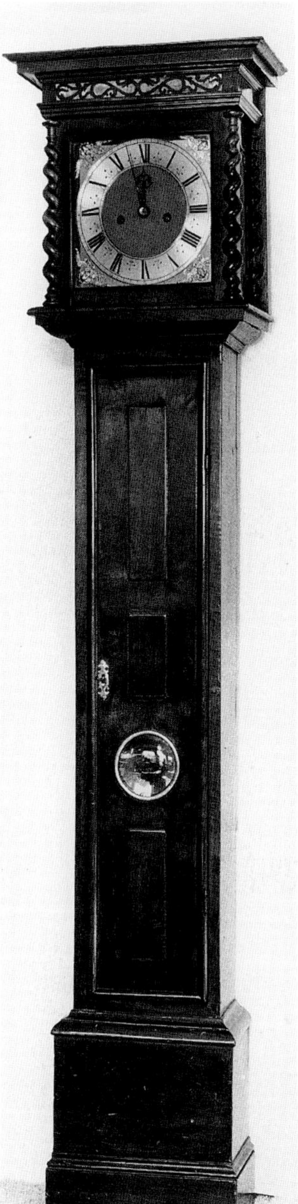

96. Ten-inch (25.5 cms) dial of an eight-day longcase clock of about 1680 made by John Wise of London. Such early dials are often very simple in styling, the absence of calendar and seconds dials making the matted centre look very plain. The winding-holes are plain (later ones being ringed), and the centre has no engraving work of any kind. Minute numbers are extremely small and lie within the double engraved line forming the minute band – within a few years the style was to have these numbers outside the band. Spandrels are of the tiny winged cherub-head type, too small for a dial larger than ten inches. The signature appears below the chapter ring on the main dial sheet; a little later signatures were positioned on the chapter ring for greater visibility when the clock was in its case. This movement has six pillars, and the four dial feet are held in place by latches instead of the pins which were used later. Half-hour markers are simple and restrained forms of fleurs-de-lis.

95. Small and slender case of the John Wise clock (96), *c.* 1680, standing only about 6 ft 3 ins (190 cms). Barley-sugar pillars are a feature of many clocks of this period, as is the fret below the hood topmould, which has a cloth backing and lets out the sound of the bell. The D-moulding (half-round moulding) on the door rim is a classic feature of most clocks of this age. The three-panel effect on the door is a feature of some clocks from this early period. The base of the case is replaced. This case is veneered in fruitwood and is a rich brown colour; some clocks of this type are veneered in ebony and are near-black. Later examples were veneered in pearwood and polished black to resemble ebony, and are known as 'ebonized'. Some were polished black without the pearwood veneer, for cheapness – ebonized pearwood looked much more like ebony than ebonized pine. Here the lenticle glass has a brass rim, more often the rim would be a wooden D-mould.

97. Ten-inch (25 cms) dial from an eight-day clock by Aaron Cheasbrough, dated 1689. This maker worked at Penrith by 1699, but may have worked earlier at nearby Ousby. This is believed to be the oldest recorded domestic Cumberland clock, certainly the oldest *dated* clock there, and the very presence of the date on the dial, an extremely unusual feature, suggests that the maker was keen to record its date for posterity. The cherub-head spandrel is of the same pattern as that used on contemporary London clocks. The confining of the minute numbers within the minute band is a feature of this time, discontinued soon after. The marking of seconds every fifth unit was normal with clocks of this age, as was the placing of the signature on the dial-sheet below the chapter ring. The matted dial centre without engraving is the same as the London fashion of the day. The style of the dial overall is based on the London style of the time, yet the engraving has not quite the expert workmanship of a London clock, so this is not simply a clock bought from London and lettered with a local name. The movement has outside countwheel control for the striking.

98. Case of the Aaron Cheasbrough clock of 1689 (97) in veneered walnut. Based on contemporary London work, yet certain features have a more provincial look to them – the barley-sugar pillars for instance are heavier than the finer lines of a London case. Height about 6 ft 8 ins (204 cms). The top-of-trunk moulding at this time has a convex shape. The veneers are bookmatched on the base, i.e. a split mirror image formed by joining two adjacent slices of veneer, one folded over to reflect the other. The door is bookmatched in three matching double sections. The lenticle (bull's-eye) glass in the door is a feature of many early clocks, as is the half-round beading edging the trunk door. The proportions of a late seventeenth century longcase such as this are quite unmistakable once a few have been seen.

99. Month-duration longcase clock in marquetry by James Girod of London dating from about 1695. This case, standing about 7 ft (213 cms), is of the type known as 'all-over' marquetry, where the marquetry fills the entire door and base rather than being in confined panels. The hood door, base surround and door frame are also marquetried, as are even some of the mouldings. The sides of such cases were normally, as here, veneered in walnut without any marquetry. Glass windows in the hood side were a feature of many London clocks – in the provinces these were only found in certain regions at certain periods. The D-mould edging the trunk door is typical of the period, and the same mould edges the lenticle glass in the door. The pierced fret, backed with cloth, immediately below the hood topmould was to allow the sound of the bell to emerge. Most month-duration clocks in London were made about this period, after which eight-day duration was considered adequate for all normal purposes and month clocks seemed to pass from fashion.

100. Twelve-inch (30.5 cms) square-dial of an eight-day longcase clock of about 1700-10 by Thomas Bradford of London. The movement has six pillars – London clocks normally had five pillars, but before about 1730 it was not uncommon for them to have more than five. The spandrel pattern shows twin cherubs holding a crown, a popular pattern at this time. The dial is edged with an engraved pattern (and a not dissimilar pattern frames the nameplate engraved into the dial-centre), known as herringbone engraving, or wheatear pattern. The winding-holes have decorative rings, a popular feature of the period and perhaps done to avoid keymarks showing up on a plain matted edge, where the winding-key may occasionally have scraped. Diamond-shaped (or lozenge) half-hour markers were used by some, though not all, makers from this time in London (later in the provinces). The smaller diamond-shaped marker indicates 'half-quarters', and the hands are just approaching 'half-quarter' past ten. Today we would call it seven (and-a-half) minutes past, but at the time those unaccustomed to clocks found measuring time by quarters and half-quarters much simpler to understand than minutes.

101. Eight-day clock by Thomas Bradford of London dating from about 1700–10 in its lacquer case, the ground-colour being blue-green. The case retains its original caddy top with gilded wooden finials and stands about 7 ft 10 ins (238 cms). Many such clocks have had the caddies removed to reduce height, but the fact that this clock retains its pediments gives it an altogether more graceful shape and proportion. The overall style is typical of London clocks of the day, and cases of this same overall shape were also made in walnut and in marquetry, but not usually in oak in London. Lacquerwork can be in badly deteriorated condition today. This example is very well-preserved, and most of the decorative giltwork can be seen to be complete. The circular window in the door is known as a lenticle glass, and is a feature of many clocks at this period. Its purpose is believed to be to show up the moving pendulum bob, which here appears out of line only because the photograph is taken from a low angle.

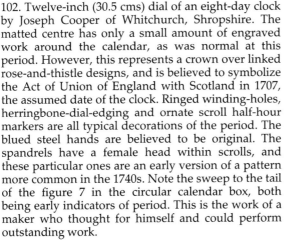

102. Twelve-inch (30.5 cms) dial of an eight-day clock by Joseph Cooper of Whitchurch, Shropshire. The matted centre has only a small amount of engraved work around the calendar, as was normal at this period. However, this represents a crown over linked rose-and-thistle designs, and is believed to symbolize the Act of Union of England with Scotland in 1707, the assumed date of the clock. Ringed winding-holes, herringbone-dial-edging and ornate scroll half-hour markers are all typical decorations of the period. The blued steel hands are believed to be original. The spandrels have a female head within scrolls, and these particular ones are an early version of a pattern more common in the 1740s. Note the sweep to the tail of the figure 7 in the circular calendar box, both being early indicators of period. This is the work of a maker who thought for himself and could perform outstanding work.

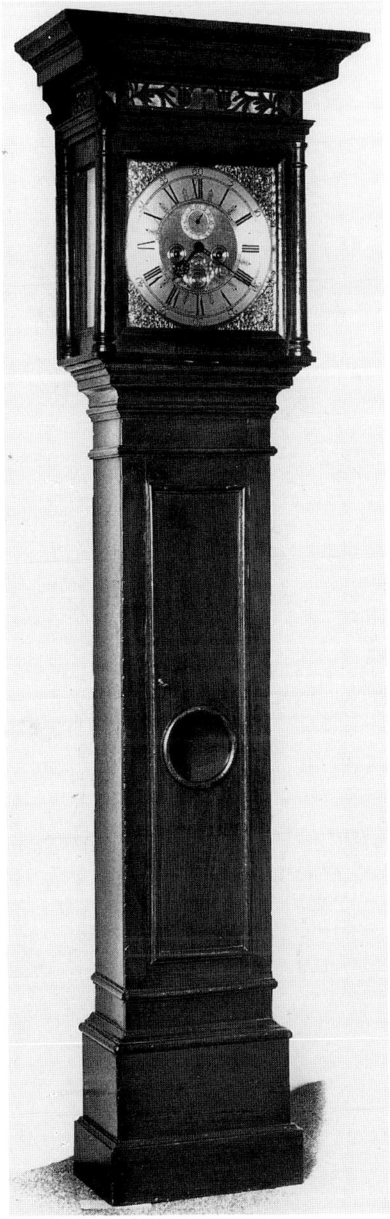

103. Interesting oak case of the Joseph Cooper clock of 1707 (102), showing some primitive, early features, yet well-preserved in good condition, with the exception that the base has probably been shortened in height and a replacement plinth fitted at some time in the past. The heavy overhang of the topmould and the very large side windows are an early sign of country work, as are pillars attached to the door on a northern clock. The flat door top is an early feature here, as is the lenticle glass. The pierced fret in the hood is heavy yet shows some character. The door has an astragal beading around its edge and more rings the case above and below the door, where there would otherwise be a blank area of trunk. As with most clocks of this age in oak, the colour can be seen to have darkened considerably with age. Height about 6 ft 3 ins (190 cms). It is amazing that such cottage clocks have survived at all considering the rough handling they must have had in imperfect conditions of accommodation.

104. Twelve-inch (30.5 cms) dial of a different eight-day clock by Joseph Cooper of Whitchurch, dating about 1705-10. Some stylistic features here are typical of the period – ringed winding-holes, round calendar box, early figures revealed by the flat-topped 8, half-quarter markers, herringbone or wheatear border engraving to the dial, matted centre with a little engraving round the date, half-hour markers meeting arrowheads in curved form, and twin-cherub pattern of spandrels, here supporting a crown. The minute hand looks original, but the hour hand seems later in style. This clock chimes the quarter-hours on three bells, without any drive power, as a lug trips a series of bladesprings in the same manner as the 'passing strike' system on many skeleton clocks of the late nineteenth century.

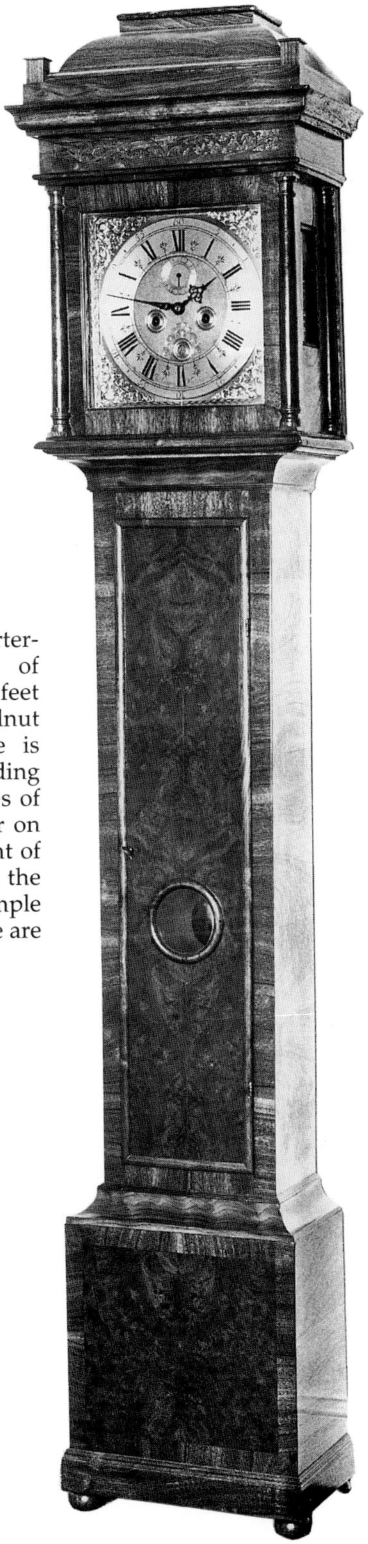

105. Walnut-veneered case (restored) of the quarter-chiming eight-day clock by Joseph Cooper of Whitchurch (104), *c.* 1705-10. The plinth and bun feet are replacements. The original caddy in solid walnut is preserved, whereas almost everything else is veneered. The door shape, and its surrounding D-mould and lenticle glass are all typical features of the period. Pillars are attached to the hood door on these early clocks and open with the door. Height of the case about 7 ft 6 ins (229 cms). By this date, the mouldings above and below the trunk are of simple concave section. The veneers to the door and base are book-matched – 4 to the base, 8 to the door.

107. Twelve-inch (30.5 cms) dial of an eight-day longcase clock made about 1710 by William Farrer of Pontefract. The original hands are in blued steel. This dial is very much up-to-date in terms of styling. The matted centre has a little engraving round the date box – here of two birds with a basket of fruit, a very popular theme. Half-hour markers are restrained fleurs-de-lis in the London manner. Quarter-units are virtually always marked at this period inside the chapter ring. Half-quarter markers are small diamonds (between 5 and 10, for example). Seconds are marked in units of five, as was the fashion at this period. Spandrels in this pattern, were used well into the 1720s. The use of the word 'Fecit' in the signature was normal at this time. In all, this is a high quality dial with some London influence, by a man who was familiar with the latest dial style.

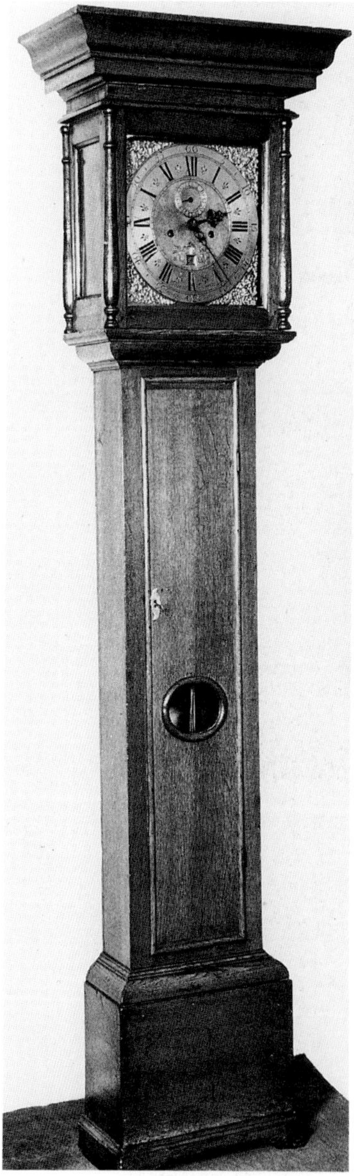

106. Oak case of the eight-day clock by William Farrer of Pontefract (107) dating from about 1710-20. The clock shows up-to-the-minute styling in its dial, the maker obviously being aware of the newest London style. The case, however, is strangely old-fashioned, yet believed original to the clock. Its overall proportion is similar to a London case of the 1690s, except that its very heavy topmould with wide overhang betrays its provincial making. The hood has very large side windows, which fill almost the whole hood sides, usually a very early sign and here a lingering feature. The attached hood pillars have a pleasing swell to them. The door has a horizontal crossmember top and bottom to prevent warping, exactly as on a London case. The D-mould around the door is typical of the period. The bracket feet are original, an unusual feature in a country clock as old as this one. Height 6 ft 10 ins (208 cms). Dial size 12 ins (30.5 cms).

108. Longcase clock of month duration made about 1715-20 by Peter King of Long Acre, London. The case is of arabesque marquetry, a myriad of small patterns based on geometrical shapes. Seaweed marquetry is similar, but with flowing, more naturalistic lines. Sometimes the words arabesque and seaweed are used indiscriminately to refer to this general type of marquetry. All kind of woods might be incorporated including holly, box, walnut, ebony, rosewood, and some woods were died to artificial colours such as green, making identification now very difficult. It was a style popular for a generation or so from about 1690 to 1720, and then only principally in London. This is a fine example with its original caddy top still preserved. The height is about 7 ft 10 ins (238 cms). Marquetry veneer is laid on these cases even in the most difficult of positions – e.g. the hood pillars are veneered and the mouldings. Very small moulds which could not possibly be marquetried were often, as here, stained to a darker colour (black sometimes) for contrast. A contemporary case in walnut (without marquetry) would have followed this same stylistic pattern.

109. Twelve-inch dial of an eight-day longcase clock by Peter King of Long Acre, London, dating from about 1715-20 – not the same clock as the marquetry one in plate 108. This dial illustrates many typical London features of the day: matted-dial-centre with square date box and a small amount of engraving around it, ringed winding-holes, flat-topped figure 8, seconds ring marked every fifth unit, meeting arrowhead half-hour markers, herringbone engraved dial edge, twin cherub spandrels holding a crown, half-quarter markers marked by a small arrowpoint. The blued steel hands are replacements, but of the correct style and based on patterns of the period. The workmanship is very good, the engraving highly skilled. The overall tone is sober, with the exception of the herringbone edging.

110. Detail of the hood of the Peter King of Long Acre clock (109), *c.* 1715-20. The original caddy top is preserved. The three-quarter pillars are attached to the hood door and open with it, whilst quarter pillars are set at the back against a straight back splat. The characteristic door top can be seen in detail, with its half-round moulding, known as a D-mould. Note that the upper door frame is veneered in book-matched manner, as well as the door itself. The top-of-the trunk moulding is not quite typical in shape, this one being an ogee curve, whereas more often by this date this mould would be a simple concave one. Glass side windows to the hood enable most of the movement to be seen from the side, the reason for it perhaps was to provide the curious with a view of the first machine in operation. The hood side windows on these clocks tend to be large, covering much of the space available. Walnut is used throughout.

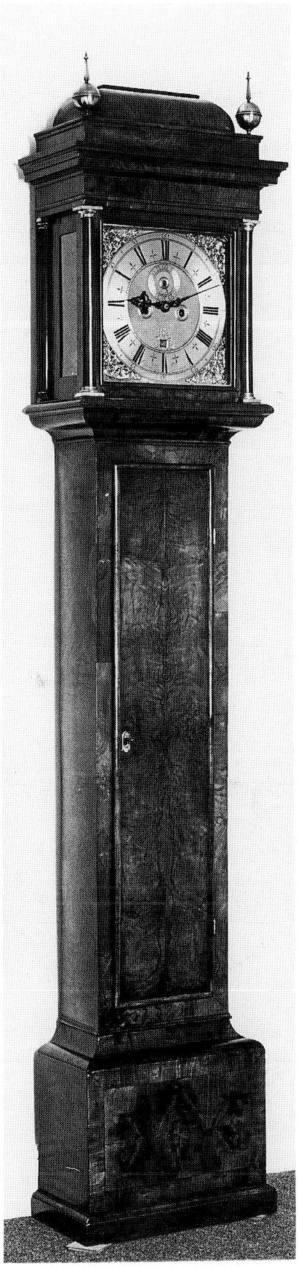

111. The case of the Peter King clock (109) of *c.* 1715-20 is in walnut with book-matched veneers to the door and base – the door is in eight panels, but these are difficult to isolate visually as the jointed areas are cut in serpentine manner to disguise them. The base is quartered (i.e. in four panels), though there has been restoration to the base, that being the part most prone to suffer from damp over the years. The long thin trunk is typical, and the long door fills all available space but for its framework. The sides of the case are veneered in sections with horizontal grain direction. The walnut veneer is laid on to an oak carcase, though sometimes the basewood is pine. The height is 7 ft 4 ins (223 cms).

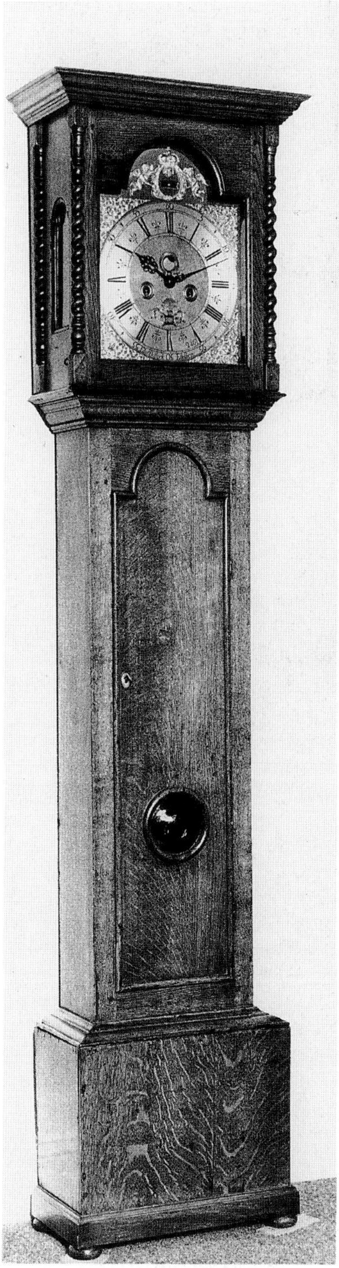

113. Arched-dial (12 ins, 30.5 cms) from an eight-day clock by Edmund Bullock of Ellesmere, Shropshire, no. 246, a maker who regularly numbered his clocks and this one dates from about 1720. The 'Halifax' type of penny moon is unusually low and unusually small, positioned very close to the hands. The arch is very small with wide shoulders to the square section, small arches (as here) are a sign of the beginnings of the arch-dial style. Behind the slot in the arch a golden ball sways as the pendulum ticks – perhaps intended to represent the sun? Ringed winding-holes and engraving round the calendar box are typical features of the day, as are the half-quarter markers. This is a fine clock by a highly competent maker who thought for himself. Oddly enough, the band inside the chapter ring marks half hours and not quarters, an eccentric feature of Bullock's work on this particular clock and not typical of him or the period.

112. Oak case of the clock by Edmund Bullock of Ellesmere (113) dating from about 1720. The lenticle glass seldom appeared on arch-dial clocks, and then only at the beginning of the arch fashion, being a carry over from square-dial fashions. The barley-sugar pillars to the hood are also a feature of early square-dial clocks, and their use here is another indication that this is the start of the arch-dial fashion. The medullary rays show up well as figuring on the oak. The plinth and bun feet are replacements, not surprising on a cottage clock of this great age. The flat top to the hood is a feature found more often on square- than arched-dial clocks. In all, this clock bears several signs of a casemaker not yet used to the new arched style, and is indicative of the transitional period. Height about 6 ft 8 ins (204 cms).

114. Eight-day clock dating from about 1720-30 by John Sanderson of Wigton, an interesting maker and one-time Quaker, who often left his dial corners without spandrels, as here. 'Memento mori' is engraved in the top two corners – meaning 'bear death in mind'. The case is of black lacquer (on to an oak carcase), sometimes called japanwork or chinoiserie. The decoration in gold is of oriental style, though done in England. The case would almost certainly be London-made, bought in originally for the clock when it was first made, as it is extremely unlikely that anyone was making japanned furniture in Cumberland at this early period. The height is about 6 ft 10 ins (208 cms). Quaker clocks (and cases) were usually of a sober nature, and the implication here is that a case of this highly ornate type would have been ordered specifically by the customer. The overall shape of the case is little different from one of this age made in oak or walnut.

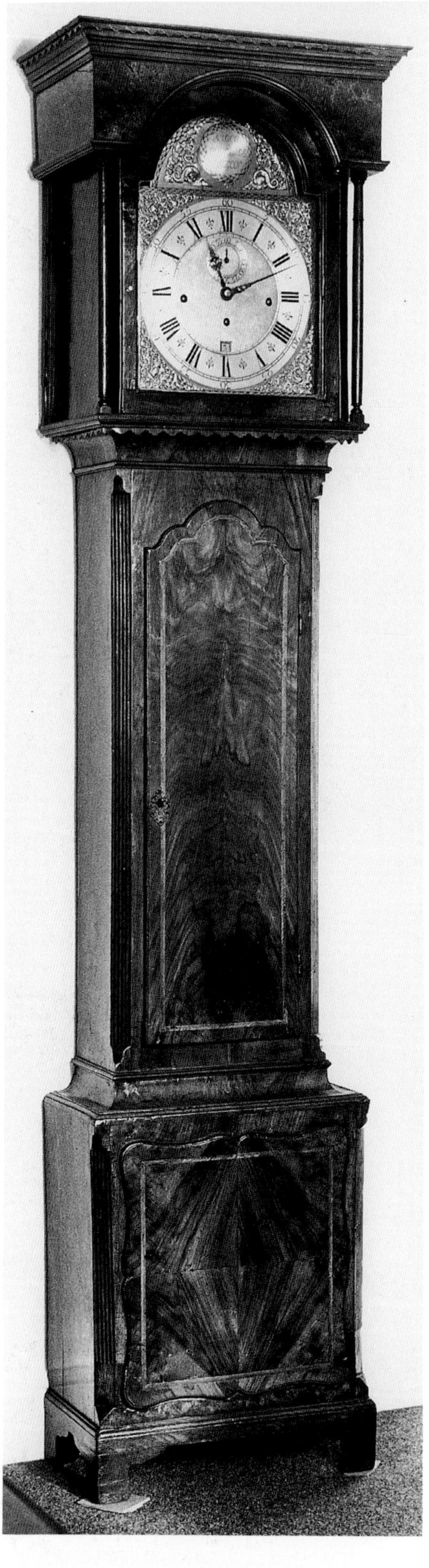

115. Case of an eight-day three-train musical clock by Jacob Lovelace of Exeter, *c.* 1730-40. The case is veneered in bookmatched walnut, the door being a double mirror image and the base being a fourfold repeat. The wavy pattern of the raised base panel is unusual, though it extends the trunk doortop shape in principle. This may be due to influence from nearby Bristol where wavy-edged panels were popular. The veneer is laid on to an oak carcase. An inlaid stringing-line is set in a short distance from the door and panel edges, though the veneer grain can be seen to continue beyond the stringing in the same pattern. The height is about 7 ft 4 ins (223 cms), the dial 12 inches across (30.5 cms). The bracket feet are replaced but in the correct style. It is debatable whether there was once some upper pediment above the flat hood top. Notice that when a three-train clock was planned originally the winding-holes are set out with symmetry; one with a hole in an eccentric or unsymmetrical position, has probably had the third train added later.

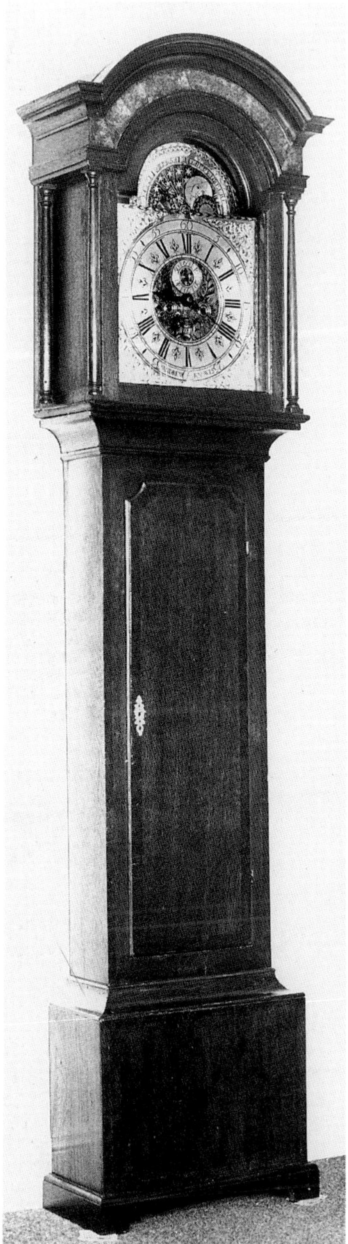

116. Dial of a longcase eight-day clock of about 1730-40 by Andrew Knowl(e)s, who worked at Bolton. The dial is surprisingly large for its date at 14 inches (38 cms), and is also surprising for its riotously bold and interesting style. The engraving is exceptionally bold and looks even stronger in this picture as the dial is in dirty condition. A herringbone-type of engraved border surrounds the dial and moon dial and moon 'humps'. The moon is engraved on to a brass disc and was silvered, as were the stars, on to a radiating sky ground – all here in need of re-silvering. All the hands are original in steel but have lost their bluing. The dial-centre has vigorous leafgrowth worked into the ringed winding-holes and date box. Bold diamonds mark the half-quarters. The spandrel pattern is that of an urn supported by two eagles. Moon dials normally show the single lunar number of the moon's 'age', but here the apertures show the lunar date in the top centre and each of the four lunar weeks around it, a most unusual treatment. Most of these features are typical of the period, but the unusually bold and exuberant style of the engraving is down to the personality of the particular maker and is not typical. The dial size too is untypical for this period. This type of moon, which fills the arch, is often known as a rolling moon.

117. Oak case of the clock by Andrew Knowl(e)s of Bolton (116), about 1730-40. It has crossbanding in walnut (edge of door and edge of base). The free-standing hood pillars are slender and taper towards the top, as is usual with examples as early as this. Rear half-pillars facing forwards are attached to back splats. Below the topmould of the domed hood is a burr wood infill – burred woods are always difficult to identify, but it is probably walnut. The bracket foot is a replacement, but of the correct style. Dome top cases such as this are unusual. Many once had a top pediment above the dome, some were later removed to reduce the overall height. This clock stands about 7 ft 10 ins (238 cms).

119. Twelve-inch (30.5 cms) dial of an eight-day longcase clock made about 1730-40 by John Taylor of Ashton-under Lyne. This is a very unusual clock in so far as it is a single-handed eight-day; virtually all single-handers were thirty-hour clocks, and less than half a dozen eight-day ones are documented in the published literature on clocks. The clock was made as an eight-day, not converted later from a thirty-hour. The blued steel hand is original and very well made with a curved thumbpiece tail for leverage when setting the time. The calendar is placed unusually at the top of the dial-centre, with ringed surround to match the winding-holes and just a hint of engraving around the circular calendar box. The engraved rim to the chapter ring is very unusual, just a whim of the maker. Half-hour markers are bold fleurs-de-lis type. Such a clock would have been made as a special order for a customer who was traditionally-minded and wanted the convenience of eight-day duration without the complexity of those confusing new-fangled two hands.

118. The oak case of the John Taylor of Ashton-under-Lyne clock (119) of about 1730-40 stands only 6 ft 4 ins (192 cms) including its original caddy top. It has its original plinth and has not been reduced in height. It was presumably made for a low ceiling. The case looks stocky by virtue of its small height combined with large dial. The slim pillars, swelling at the lower section, are typical of this period in the north, being free-standing, and the door top shape is also typical of this period. The hinges barely show, but are of wrought iron 'butterfly' type, as are the hood door hinges, which cannot be seen in the photograph. The moulding shapes and the caddy top shape are pure north-western.

120. Twelve-inch (30.5 cms) dial of an eight-day longcase clock made between 1730 and 1740 by William Stumbels of Totnes, a very fine clockmaker. The blued steel hands are original throughout. The corner spandrels of two eagles supporting an urn are typical of this period. Dolphin-pattern arch spandrels were used over a long period. The herringbone border used in this clock was a little old-fashioned by this date. All the engraving work is crisp and of the best quality, yet restrained (as e.g. the small half-hour marker) compared to some northern work. The dial in the centre of the arch shows the moon's age on the outer band of numbers (1-29½) and tide times on the inner band (I-XII twice). The indicators on this dial are set out to resemble the two hands of a clock dial. Such a tidal dial can be used to read high water at any port. Once the tide time is set relative to the moon's age, then the two pointers move round in the same relationship to each other. This is known as a universal tidal dial. The switch below this dial is to run the clock with or without strikework, as required. This is very fine work by one of the best provincial makers.

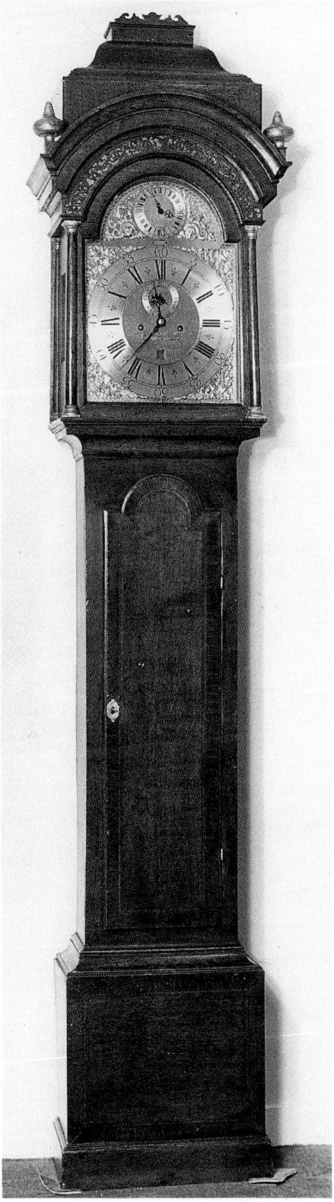

121. Oak case of the clock by William Stumbels of Totnes (120) *c.* 1730-40. The height is about 8 ft (244 cms). This clock retains its original caddy above the dome section and its original crested box top. The two gilded wooden finials are believed original. The bracket foot is probably a replacement, as it lacks any style. The oak is crossbanded in quite a wide strip of walnut, separated by a light stringing-line. This shows particularly on the door and base. The fretwork beneath the hood dome is in good condition. Glass side windows in the hood are a feature often retained in the south, but seldom appear as late as this in northern England (though they do in Scotland). Being on the tall side enables this clock to retain its elegance of line. The case style is somewhat simpler and plainer than a contemporary northern one, which would have more complex mouldings and shapings.

123. Twelve-inch (30.5 cms) dial of an eight-day longcase clock of the 1730s by Peter Green of Liverpool who went to live in Denmark in 1744. 'Liverpool' is here spelt in the old way as 'Leverpool'. Here the arch section is a separate construction joined to the square, and was made that way originally (though this can sometimes be an indication of an altered clock). The engraving is of very high quality and bold in style. Note the half-quarter markers and the very fine birds engraved into the matted dial-centre. The hands are of blued steel and are original. Note the idiosyncratic manner of engraving the 1 in 10, 15, etc., and the flowery crossbar on the 4, all signs of an engraver with a little individuality of thought, and indications of quality of execution. Note the flat-topped figure 8 in the calendar box, a frequent feature at this period.

122. The fine walnut case of the clock by Peter Green of Liverpool (123). Door and base panel are in bookmatched veneers, all crossbanded in walnut. This is the only veneer to the case, the rest of which is in solid timber. The panel beneath the hood topmould is of 'verre églomisé', that is a glass panel, painted on the back with a body colour (here blue) and on the surface with gold scrollwork. Such a glass panel became a popular feature on many Lancashire clocks from this time on, and was an alternative to a pierced sound-fret. The height of the clock is about 7 ft 2 ins (219 cms). The hood pillars are free-standing, a feature which occurred earlier in the north than in the south, where hood pillars at this time would still be integral with the hood door.

124. Thirteen-inch (33 cms) dial of an eight-day longcase clock made about 1730-40 by Thomas Ogden of Halifax, a very fine clockmaker. An unusual feature, but a favourite with Ogden, was a half-round brass beaded edge to his dial-sheets, as here. Its presence is essentially decorative, but it probably also adds strength against bending, though dial-sheets would seldom bend unless dropped. The female head corner spandrels are typical of the period; dolphin spandrels in the arch cover a wide time span. In the arch is a form of penny moon dial, the moon's shape depicted by a silvered disc with silvered stars on a black-waxed sky. The moon's age is shown by a hand, which turns on the same post as the moon disc. The engraved floral centre to the moon feature is especially fine. A bold fleur-de-lis marks the half-hours; a smaller marks the half-quarters. The dial-centre is matted. Applied decorative rings are attached to cover the winding-holes and circular calendar box; these are another favourite feature of this maker, as most ringed winding-holes are ringed into the dial-sheet itself. Two small holes can be seen on the inner chapter ring at III and IX. These are not rivets for the chapter ring, but are probably rivet positions used when the ring was fixed to a turntable during engraving. This maker would never dream of riveting his chapter ring to the dial-sheet, a sign of the work of a lesser maker than Ogden.

125. Oak case of the clock by Thomas Ogden of Halifax (124), *c.* 1730-40. A large starburst (or sunburst, as it is sometimes called) decorates the door centre and base centre, being of alternate dark and light wood inlays. Starbursts are a feature of some clocks, mostly northern, about this time. A black-and-yellow chequered string-line separates the walnut crossbanding on the hood door, trunk door and base. The hood retains its caddy top above the dome section. Most northern clocks have free-standing hood pillars by this date. A shaped top is a feature of the doors of many northern clocks. A burr-walnut infill fronts the flat section below the hood-dome moulding. Note the busy mould joining the trunk to the base, very different from a simple concave mould on a southern clock. Total height is about 8 ft (244 cms). A narrow D-mould decorates the edge of the trunk door, this is not just for decoration but also helps cover any gap caused by shrinkage.

126. Oak case of the Tantum clock (127), standing 7 ft 4 ins (223 cms). The crossbanding is in walnut. Inlaid roundels of varicoloured woods centre on a starburst in the door centre and base panel. Dot-dash chequerwork-stringing surrounds base, door and hood door and is also lined beneath the hood pediment, this shape of a dome with a cut-away centre being usually known as a break-arch. Hood pillars are integral with the door. Glass side windows to the hood in this example are an indication of the period. Pillar capitals are of gilded wood, as was often the case with country clocks.

127. Twelve-inch (30.5 cms) dial of an eight-day longcase clock of 1730-40 by Daniel Tantum of Loscoe, Derbyshire. Little is known about the life of this maker, but the quality of his clocks is usually high. The spandrels are a mask-head pattern popular at this period. Note the half-quarter markers (e.g. between 5 and 10) which are unusually bold and also the bold half-hour markers. The blued steel hands are original. The mouth-type calendar is here unusually large and, oddly, the number of the date shows through a smaller box below the hands fitting. The engraved scrolls into the matted centre twine purposely around the winding-holes. Quarter-hour units are marked inside the chapter ring, typical of the period.

128. Magnificent dial of the musical clock by William Stumbels (130), *c.* 1740. This clock plays 'Worship the King' every third hour, though a chime can be played instead. The change switch is on the right by 15. The arch carries a revolving ball moon feature as well as a high-tide indicator. The workmanship is superb throughout with fine engraved scrollwork running into and around the spandrels. Though there are only two winding-holes, this is a three-train clock, and employs Stumbels's own system for winding the concealed third train. The blued steel hands are believed original. This highly complex clock was supplied with hand-written instructions from the maker pasted inside the case door – which survive to this day. Twelve-inch (30.5 cms) dial.

129. The movement of the Stumbels musical clock (128), the dial removed, and pictured here in its dirty condition before cleaning. The third, central train is hidden but is wound by using the specially cut 'tail' of the winding-key, which slots into the gear *outside* the right-hand winding-square, winding through an intermediate wheel to the concealed mainwheel. The musical section can be seen on the upper right, with its tune selection switch protruding. Note the great amount of wheelwork here competing for space, among which the hour-striking work of rack and snail can be made out clearly. This photograph was taken in 1988, when the clock had not been cleaned since 1914, yet it was still in running order, although it had lain disused for many years.

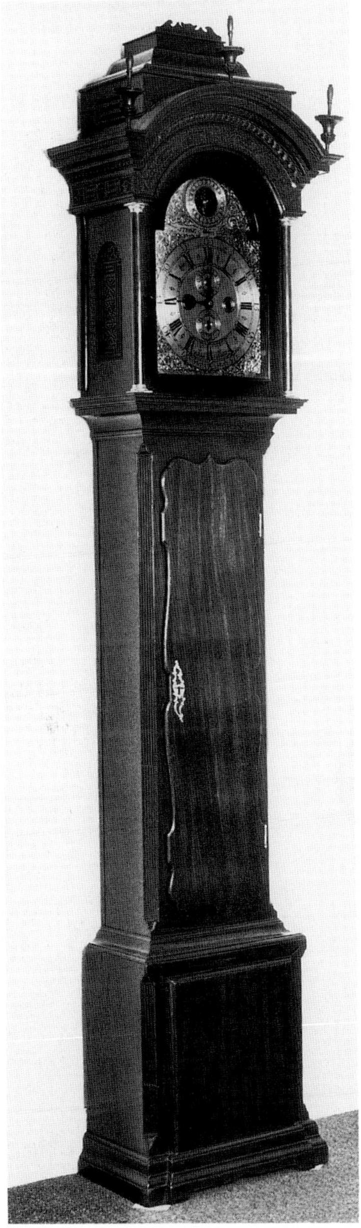

130. Highly complicated and very important eight-day longcase clock made about 1740 by William Stumbels of Totnes, Devon (128). The case is a very early example of the use of mahogany. It stands just over eight ft high (244 cms) and has its original multiple caddy above the dome. The wavy-edged trunk door shows influence from Bristol, on which this sort of door-shaping centred as a style. Note the unusual break-front plinths. Sound frets in the hood side and upper caddy side are to let out the sound of this musical clock. Note the fine flambeau-style finials. This is a very grand clock, and, must have been extremely costly in its day.

132. Thirteen-inch (33 cms) square dial of an eight-day longcase clock by William Davenport of Stockport dating from about 1740-50. The blued steel hands are original. Here the spandrel pattern is the large Lancashire cherub-head type, often used on arched dials. Half-hour markers are small diamonds, unusually small for this region, but perhaps in this instance done small because of the place-names engraved between the hour numbers. The matted centre has considerable scroll engraving worked into it (designed to wrap around the winding-holes and incorporate them into the pattern); this engraving on to a matted ground is a stylistic feature confined mostly to north-western England. The place-names engraved round the dial form a simple kind of world-time dial. A dot within each hour division and engraved into the inner chapter ring circle, indicates that when the hour hand touches that point, it is noon in the place named above. For instance, just after 12.30 here is noon in Cadiz; 1.50 here is noon in the Cape Verde Islands, and so on. A world-time dial is very unusual, but this one is so limited in its use that it is difficult to see what purpose it might have served – other than to impress the neighbours.

131. The oak case of the William Davenport of Stockport clock (132), the style being typical of the north-west at this period – 1740s. The case retains its original caddy top, the front of which is pierced with decorative holes to let the bell sound through. The raised base panel with clipped corners matches the clipped corner shape of the trunk door top, and is a typical north-western feature. Most clocks in the north by this time had free-standing hood pillars, as this one has, though the pillars are slender and graceful with considerable thinning and taper towards their tops. The ornate brass escutcheon plate is original. The quarter-columns flanking the trunk appear on many clocks from this time forward, especially in the north. The height is about 7 ft (213 cms). The bracket foot is original.

133. Eight-day clock dating from about 1740 by John Ettry of Bishop's Canning, Wiltshire, here written as 'Bpp:CANNONS.' Spelling often varied at the discretion of the engraver. The maker was not born till 1717, and so the clock cannot date before the late 1730s, though some stylistic features might at first suggest it was older. The half-quarter marker is not often retained as late as this, and the twin cherubs with crossed maces and large crown, which form the spandrel pattern, were normally used earlier than this. The matted dial-centre with a little engraving around the calendar box was used throughout the second quarter of the century. The hands are believed replacements and cannot be used as a guide to period, though they are in the correct sort of style – the hour hand is perhaps a bit over-ornate for a country maker. The minute numbers are very small relative to the hours, and are also a somewhat archaic feature by this time. The dial is 11 ins (28 cms) square. The hour numerals and half-hour fleur-de-lis markers are particularly bold, something a little unusual for a southern clock. Engraved birds-with-a-basket in the dial-centre is a theme which occurs in varying forms throughout a wide area in central southern England and the Midlands.

134. Oak case of the clock by John Ettry of Bishop's Canning (133), with the figured medullary rays showing plainly (produced when oak was quarter-cut). This simple, country case retains features which were a little old-fashioned by 1740. The very slender shape, and the D-mould round the door and lenticle grass are features more often found earlier, but retained, as here, in some country clocks. The wrought-iron H-hinges show well. The base has been shortened and, therefore, looks disproportionally low. Pillars attached to the hood door, as here, were used much longer in the south than in the north, where clocks by this time usually had free-standing pillars. Height about 6 ft (183 cms).

135. Thirteen-inch (33 cms) dial, with moon and tidal features in the arch, from an eight-day clock of about 1745 made by Jonas Barber of Winster, Westmorland. This maker numbered his clocks, of which this is number 78. The narrow herringbone edging is unusual both in nature and in being used as late as this. The work is of a very high standard. Note the pigtail 5, a feature of this maker's work. The seconds (centre-seconds) hand is a replacement, but the main hands, of blued steel, are original and exceptionally fine. The wavy minute band, often called a 'Dutch' minute band, was used on occasion by some makers in mid-century, usually in the north. The moon dial has the lunar date on the outer edge, high-water times inside that. The blue, starry sky background was normal on early moon dials.

136. Twelve-inch (30.5 cms) dial from an eight-day clock by William Porthouse of Penrith. This is actually dated 1750, and bears the names in the plaque in the arch of the first owners, William and Margaret Fawcet. The clock was probably a wedding present, known as a 'marriage clock'. This particular maker often used to include the first owners' names and sometimes the year. The corner spandrels are the two eagles supporting an urn, with dolphins in the arch. The dial is photographed here in unrestored condition, some tarnishing being obvious. Half hours are marked by a large fleur-de-lis but quarter-hour units have now ceased to appear. The blued steel hands are of non-matching pattern and could well be original. The maker's name is engraved on a plaque, a method this maker often used, and merely an alternative to the more usual way of signing his name on the chapter ring.

137. Twelve-inch (30.5 cms) dial from an eight-day longcase clock of about 1750 by James Wilson of Askrigg, North Yorkshire. This dial is photographed in dirty condition – note the blackened metal polish in the spandrels, which have an Indian head theme, and are typical of this period, though little used in the north. The arch spandrels are dolphins, between which a penny moon feature seems curiously too small for the available space. The steel hands are original. The calendar disc rotates against a pointer below the hands, broken away in this picture. Note the primitive graining in the matted centre. Half hours are marked by diamonds, but by this time quarter-hour marking had fallen out of fashion. The signed nameplate is fixed crookedly because a rivet has broken. The engraving is good, but the matting is poor, and it is possible this may have been scratched by rough attempts at cleaning.

138. Thirteen-inch (33 cms) dial of an eight-day longcase clock by David Collier of Gatley (Green), Cheshire, dating from about 1750. The rolling moon has painted scenes between the moon faces with engraved and silvered numbers around its perimeter, and is read off by the pointer at the top – here half-way through the twenty-third lunar day. The spandrel is the large 'Lancashire' cherub-head pattern much used in mid-century in this area, usually on 13-inch dials. Half-hour markers and inner quarter-hour divisions to the chapter ring were still in use in mid-century. The engraving is good and sharp and the dial-centre is especially well done. This north-western style has a matted ground with engraving into it, the winding-holes and calendar box are often worked into the pattern, as here. The blued steel hands are believed original. The recessed seconds dial has a scalloped border to catch the eye and a compass rose pattern on its centre. A fine dial.

139. Oak case crossbanded with walnut of the clock by David Collier of Gatley (138), *c.* 1750. Beneath the top mould of the dome top is a frieze with painted scroll decoration in gold. These are usually painted on to a blue-green background (some are on to a glass panel, but are subject to breakage), and was a painted representation of what was on some clocks a pierced fret. A simpler case than some north-western ones of the day. Canted lower trunk mouldings were popular in this area, as was the canted-corner base. Here the plinth is a replacement of what may originally have been bracket feet, or a plinth shaped into a bracket foot. The height is about 7 ft 8 ins (234 cms). The walnut banding is round the edge of the door, which was the normal position, but on the base it can be seen to be set well in from the edge, probably to represent a base-panel effect. The banding does not appear to have ever run across the lower part of the base; and it is not uncommon for crossbanding to run along the top and both sides of a base without crossing at the bottom, even on bases which have not been shortened.

140. Dial of a 12-inch (30.5 cms) eight-day longcase clock by John Coates of Tetbury dating from about 1750. The quality is good, though some of the stylistic features are unusual. The chapter ring has the wavy minute band known as a 'Dutch' minute band (as some Dutch clocks have them), and is a feature used on occasion by makers, mostly from the north. Small and restrained fleur-de-lis markers indicate the half hours, as does a dot on the inner chapter ring edge. Quarter-hour units are not marked at all. The matted centre has engraving around the calendar box of the common birds-with-basket-of-fruit theme. The dolphin-arch spandrel was used over a long period, but the corner ones of two eagles supporting an urn was only used for about twenty years. In the arch cut-out Father Time rocks as the clock ticks, against the background of a starry sky. The hour hand has had its loops removed (perhaps to disguise breakage) and the minute hand is a modern copy. The seconds hand could well be original. A curious mixture of some rather old-fashioned stylistic features and some up-to-date ones.

141. Twelve-inch (30.5 cms) dial of an eight-day clock of the 1760s by Edward Rudd of Melksham. By this time the half-hour and quarter-hour markers had fallen from fashion, giving the chapter ring a much plainer appearance than on earlier clocks. Here the dial-centre is engraved with pillars and scrolls on to a polished background, but in some examples actual buildings appear complete, almost like a small townscape. The spandrel pattern is based on a head with a ruff, and was popular at this period. This pattern often seems to be poorly finished, though in this example the spandrels are well cast and cleaned crisply from any casting rag. The hands are believed original. The seconds dial cuts into the chapter ring in a rather odd way, though obviously this was intentional. A smaller seconds dial would have achieved the same result without clipping the chapter ring. The mouth calendar is unusual since it was not much used in eight-day work, it required one wheel less to drive it than the box type.

142. Twelve-inch (30.5 cms) dial of an eight-day longcase clock made about 1760 by James Ivory of London (who moved to Dundee about 1762). A standard London dial of the second half of the century. The matted centre is quite plain, as is the chapter ring, which by now has ceased to carry half-hour or quarter-hour divisions. The recessed seconds dial has a scalloped edge, though not all do. Seconds calibration every tenth unit rather than every fifth generally indicates that the style is later than mid-century. A strike/silent lever in the arch was very popular in London and to a lesser degree in the south-east, but is uncommon in the north. The spandrel pattern was commonly used in the north at this time on thirty-hour clocks, though it did not appear so often on London clocks. They are original. The hands are believed original throughout and are of blued steel. A standard London dial might have looked very similar to this even twenty-five years later.

143. A classic London mahogany case of the pagoda-style housing the clock by James Ivory of London (142), *c.* 1760. This is the better type of pagoda case where the reeded hood pillars have brass wire inserts one third of their lower length, and the same treatment applies to the trunk quarter-columns. These cases were of very fine workmanship, with the best flame veneers used for the door and base panel, the rest mostly in solid wood. The height is about 8 ft (244 cms). These clocks normally have a double plinth, as here, the lower one sometimes shaped into a bracket foot. Glass side windows to the hood are normal, though some have pierced sound frets in wood, occasionally in brass. The fret to the hood front is usually of wood, cloth-backed, but some are of brass. Three spire finials to the hood was normal; often the centre one was removed later to reduce height. A great many of these cases have been cut short in recent years by removing the pagoda and leaving a sort of 'dome-top' hood, but this is usually very obvious as the proportions of the case are destroyed.

145. Twelve-inch (30.5 cms) dial from an eight-day longcase clock of about 1760-70 by William Wallen of Henley. This is very much a southern style, with matted centre showing no engraved work, and very plain, even formal, chapter ring, which by this date carries no half- or quarter-hour markers. The seconds dial is marked every tenth unit; earlier ones are marked every fifth one. The spandrels are a scrollwork style of this period. The original hands are of blued steel. Absence of ringing to the winding-holes gives a very plain appearance. Two small screws show in the matting each side of the calendar box. These are retaining screws from behind the dial which hold the two runners in position for the calendar disc; a better-planned layout would have enabled these to be concealed, perhaps behind the chapter ring. The work is of good quality, but shows little individual character.

144. Simple oak cottage-style case of the eight-day clock of about 1760-70 by William Wallen of Henley (145). The pillars are attached to the hood door, a feature continued much later in the south than in the north. The trunk is long and slim with a flat-topped door, a shape seldom seen in the north at this time. All the mouldings are simple with the exception of a little dentil moulding towards the top of the hood. There is little figure to this oak, though it is quarter-cut. The medullary rays were not always wild and strongly prominent, much depended on the individual tree and the actual angle of cutting. The bead to the base which forms a simulated panel is a little unusual, and should not to be taken as a typical feature.

146. Twelve-inch (30.5 cms) dial from an eight-day longcase clock by Richard Hackett of Harringworth, Northamptonshire, *c.* 1770–80. This has many features the other Hackett clock has – centre calendar, centre seconds, multi-tide moon dial. The blued steel hands are original. The calendar hand is of the type more frequently used for an hour hand. Scroll spandrels, plainer chapter ring (lacking half- and quarter-hour markers), engraved scenes to the moon 'humps', and scroll-and-birds centre engraving themes, are all features of this period. Here the tidal dial reads for three points at the one time, incorporating four ports. On this example the moon dial is painted, with engraved numbers to its rim. The calculation of the tidal calibrations may appear complex, but published tidal tables could be bought at this period. The moon drive is a simple twelve-hourly knock-on system, as most are. It is interesting to see two clocks by the same maker with such unusual features.

147. An interesting eight-day clock with 12-inch (30.5 cms) dial made between 1760 and 1770 by Richard Hackett of Harringworth, Northamptonshire. This has both centre seconds hand and centre calendar; the hands may well be original, but if not are of original style, and seconds and calendar hands are visually distinguishable from the time hands. The bird-and-scrollwork theme engraved in the centre is typical of this (Chippendale) period. The two moon 'humps' are engraved with tiny landscape scenes, a feature more of the south than the north, but a little unusual anywhere. The moon dial incorporates a tidal dial, which in itself is a simple enough feature. Here, however, it is calibrated to read high water at six named ports. Why the owner of a clock inland should want such features is unknown, but clockmakers made what they were asked to make. The moon is an engraved disc with moon face and stars silvered, and the area in between is waxed in black to form a night sky. Half- and quarter-hour division have by this time ceased to appear on the chapter ring, which on this example is crowded enough anyway.

148. Eight-day longcase clock with circular brass dial made about 1770 by Agar of Malton, Yorkshire. The dial is of the single-sheet type, but is marked out fully as if having a separate chapter ring. The case is of oak with mahogany crossbanding and mahogany quarter-circles in the hood door, in an attempt to conceal the awkwardness of having a circular dial within a square hood door. The hood top has a sort of pagoda caddy, an unusual variation as the pagoda top was more often used with an arched dial. The blued steel hands are original. Some makers had a particular preference for round dials, as was the case with this maker.

149. Twelve-inch (30.5 cms) dial of an eight-day longcase clock made about 1770 by Archibald Lawrie of Carlisle. The manner of lettering sometimes causes such a name to be misread as Lanrie, the old w being shaped more like a modern n. Here the engraved centre decoration is laid on to a polished ground rather than a matted one, a style more often associated with the north-east than the north-west. Some of Lawrie's dials are known to have been engraved at Newcastle upon Tyne – Thomas Bewick worked on Lawrie's dials during his apprenticeship as an engraver there, but it is impossible to say whether this was one such. The blued steel hands are original and typical of the day. Notice that the ends of the winding-squares are fancy-filed, like a four-leaf clover – a sign of a craftsman showing off his style. The corner spandrels are an uncommon form of scrollwork around a plaque. In the arch are the ubiquitous dolphin spandrels. In the centre of the arch is an old oil-painted landscape, believed original, and perhaps representing Carlisle. By this date half-hour and quarter-hour markers are no longer shown.

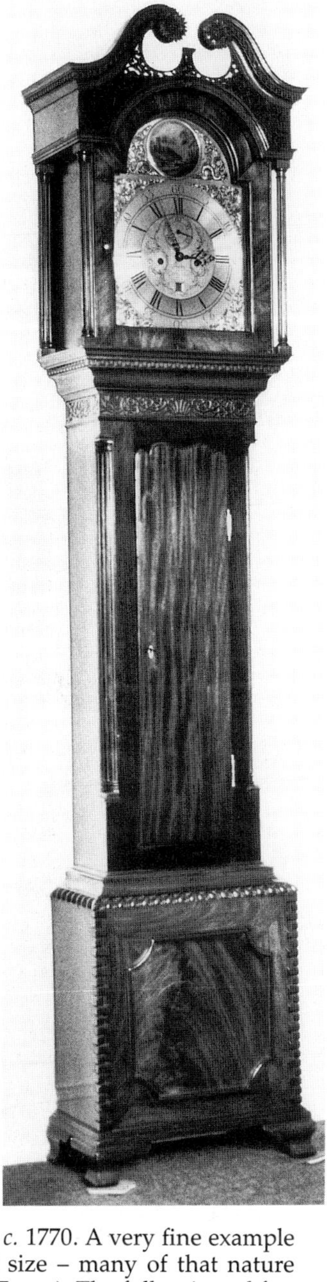

150. Mahogany case of the clock by Lawrie of Carlisle, *c.* 1770. A very fine example illustrating some Chippendale style features in small size – many of that nature stand much higher than this does at about 7 ft 5 ins (227 cms). The fully-pierced fret beneath the swan-necks, the carved swan-neck rosettes, the dentil mould beneath the hood, the fret above the door … all these represent the same sort of influence as inspired Chippendale himself. The gadrooned mould below the trunk is unusual on any longcase. The brickwork-raised pattern each side of the base is a feature most often met with in Liverpool clocks, and is known as a brickwork base. The ogee bracket feet are believed original. Reeded hood pillars are repeated at the back with forward-facing half-rounds, echoed by reeded quarter-columns to the trunk. High quality work in small stature – a scarce combination.

152. Twelve-inch (30.5 cms) dial of an eight-day longcase clock of about 1775 made by partners Allan How and Robert Knox at Irvine, Scotland. The dial-centre is a theme used principally by certain makers in eastern Scotland the background is very close-matted like a fine sandpaper finish into which is engraved lavish scrollwork. Here the pattern works very much around the calendar box. The foliate starburst in the seconds dial centre adds to this effect, as do the 3 and 5 numerals with their eccentric scrollings. The blued steel hands are believed original. By this date the half-hour markers have ceased to appear. The dolphin spandrels are still being used for the arch area as much as fifty years after their first introduction. The corner spandrels are a loosely cast cherub-head, but a version used often on clocks of lesser quality, although on this clock the engraved work is of the highest order. By this date seconds calibration is often every tenth second, instead of every fifth. Note the crack appearing in the dial-plate above the 60. The seconds dial is recessed here, and has a sort of sunray scalloped edging to its surround.

151. Case of the clock by How and Knox of Irvine (152). This is in solid mahogany, far less spectacular figuring than was possible with veneers. Even so, this wood is finely marked. It is of very small height, being only about 7 ft 2 ins (219 cms), and cannot, therefore, have the graceful and slender proportions a taller clock might have. The swan-neck pediment was probably the commonest shape of any on longcase clocks after about 1760. Here the swan-neck proportion is much like a typical English clock, though some Scottish examples are very different in balance. The grain of the wood in the base runs horizontally, which seems to be a feature of some Scottish clocks, whereas most English ones tend to have vertical grain, but this is not a firm rule. The ogee bracket feet are either original, or, if replacements, are in the correct style. The shape of the door top is very similar to the kind of shape used on some clocks from northern England. The hood pillars on this clock, and some others from this area, stand forward on projections, an odd construction, which prevents the hood door from opening more than 90 degrees. This door on the hood happens to be a left-hand opener – most hood and trunk doors open to the right.

153. A fine and most unusual dial from an eight-day longcase clock by William Wilkinson of Leeds dating from about 1780, dial 13 ins (33 cms). Some features typical of the period are large scroll spandrels, scroll engraving to the dial-centre with birds. A moon dial is set, rather unusually, above VI, the reason being that the maker in this instance wanted to use the arch for an annual calendar dial. In principle this is simply a calendar disc which moves on one point per day. Its calibration is such however that it shows below XII the day and month and any saint's day within it. The same disc shows in the arch, where several bands of information are engraved around and are read off day by day against the pointer. This shows the planetary conjunctions, sunrise time (here seven o'clock), sunset time (here five o'clock), and, closest to the disc-centre, the 'equation of time' as it is called. This latter shows how many minutes fast or slow of solar time (sundial time) one must set the clock to register mean time at any particular date. Here it shows one minute 'after', which means the clock must be set one minute later than sundial time. By this time half-hour markers on the chapter ring had fallen from fashion. The busily engraved rim to the chapter ring is a whim of the maker.

154. Oak case with mahogany trim of the annual calendar clock by William Wilkinson of Leeds (153), *c.* 1780. The hood-top shape is known as a break arch, being rather like a dome-top but with a cut-out in the centre, usually, as here, to take a finial. Mahogany is used around the base panel, around the door frame and inset on the door edge, and on the hood door and below the topmould, typical of many Leeds cases, which are distinctive in style. The hood-pillars and quarter-pillars on the trunk are in mahogany and are grooved, strictly-speaking this is known as fluting, but it is commonly referred to as reeding. Half-pillars face forwards at the back of the hood. Reeded pillars are a feature of a great many clockcases from the last quarter of the century. The bracket feet are original and are at the front only. Such a clock leaned against the wall, and the absence of rear feet is a feature quite often met with, particularly in the north-east of England. Height about 7 ft 8 ins (234 cms). The medullary ray figuring is especially obvious on the door.

155. Thirteen-inch (33 cms) dial of an eight-day clock with moonwork and annual central calendar feature made about 1790 by William Lister of Halifax. The clock also has a day-of-the-week dial above VI. Annual calendar and day-of-the-week dials are both unusual features. Note the dial-centre engraving works the winding-holes into the design. The dotted minutes are a period indicator. There is no separate chapter ring as such, it is made in one integral piece with the dial centre and this was a feature of this maker's work, adding overall strength to the dial. The name 'Jas.Greend.' is engraved below XII, probably an abbreviation for James Greenwood, who may have been the first owner of the clock. The spandrels are an unusual variation of flower and scrolls.

56. Mahogany longcase dating from about 1780-90 ·y Peter Fearnley of Wigan. The height is about 7 ft 8 ıs (234 cms). These later northern brass-dial clocks ·ften have large dials, as here, 13 inches being usual 33 cms) and 14 (38 cms) not uncommon, even on a quare dial. This means that unless the case is very all, they can look stocky. The quality of cabinetwork · amongst the best ever produced. This case is nostly in solid wood, veneer only used for radial ffect (e.g. around the base panel, above the trunk 'oor, etc.) The turned wooden finials are original and f a pattern seldom seen outside the north-west; I call nem Lancashire flying-saucer pattern, as they have o recognized name. The dial has scroll engraving to ne centre, moon work below XII, and the wider, late hapter ring, marking minutes by dots (a late feature ı brass dials). The ogee bracket feet are original. A lass panel frieze below the swan-neck was once ·ont-painted in gold, now visibly worn. The unk-to-base moulding is a complex ogee pattern vith canted corners – a style much favoured in the egion.

158. Detail of the clock by Lot Barwise of Cockermouth (157), *c.* 1780. The 13-inch (33 cms) dial has a centre calendar, the date numbers engraved on the outer edge of the dial-centre. Minutes are marked by dots, a late feature on brass dials. Below XII are the initials of the first (unknown) owners. JNJ, probably husband and wife. This was a feature of some clocks in this area, and may indicate it was made as a wedding present. Such clocks are often known as marriage clocks (a clock which is a 'marriage' is a very different thing, being made from non-original parts.) The hands are original, the calendar hand being of brass to distinguish it from the time hands. The scrollwork spandrel is more often used in the south than in this area. In the arch is a coat of arms, which has been traced and represents the arms of the Company of Stonemasons; the first owner is therefore assumed to have been a master mason. Carved flower-heads decorate the swan-neck terminals, a popular north-western feature.

157. A fine longcase clock dating from about 1780 made by Lot Barwise of Cockermouth, the case in red walnut (American walnut) and standing about 7 ft 5in (227 cms). This uncommon wood (less unusual in the north-west) is easily confused with mahogany. This case is also crossbanded in walnut. The shape, proportion, mouldings and most of its features such as clip-corner base panel, shaped doortop, ogee feet (front feet only; it never had rear feet) are very typical of this area and period. This timber probably came into the north-western ports from America, and is regarded as scarcer than mahogany, partly because it is vulnerable to woodworm attack, though less so than European walnut. It is normally used in solid form, the figure not being lively enough for veneer work. Like many clocks from the north-west, little brasswork is used on the case – pillar capitals, swan-neck terminals, etc., being of wood.

159. View of a conventional eight-day clock with its dial removed, here showing the frontplate. The rack and snail, rack spring, and gathering pallet all show clearly. Note that several of the pieces are shaped for decorative effect, even though this work would never be seen by anyone other than another clockmaker. This is a sign of high quality work, though the clock is an ordinary one. Note the four holes for the attachment of the dial by its feet; the lower left-hand hole was awkwardly close to the movement pillar, and the maker has cut this square to assist his dial fitting. The movement pillars are held in place by taper pins, which was the method normally used on all clocks. Date about 1790.

160. View of the frontplate of an eight-day clock of about 1790 made by Thomas Radford of Leeds. Most of the front wheelwork has been removed to show the engraving on the frontplate, which of course was normally quite plain. This is trial engraving, or practice engraving, perhaps done by an apprentice, but certainly of very accomplished nature. Brass was costly, and clockmakers could not afford to waste it on practice work. The scrollwork is very well done, as is the lettering. The wording 'Labor om ...' is part of the phrase 'Labor omnia vincit', meaning 'Work conquers all things'. It is not uncommon to find a little practice lettering, but this amount of hidden engraving is very unusual.

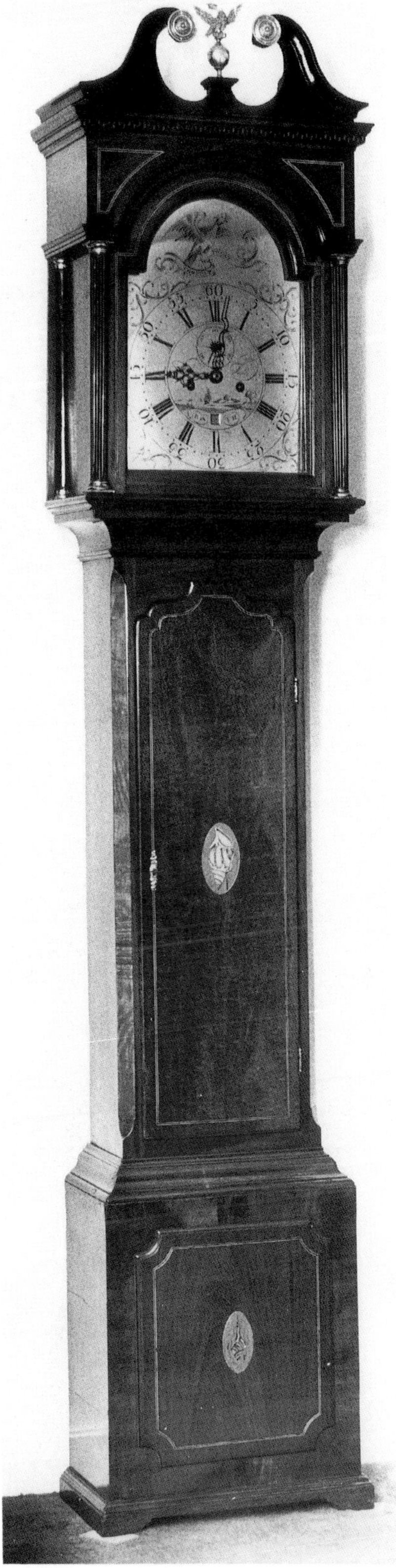

161. Mahogany case of an eight-day longcase clock with silvered single-sheet dial made about 1790 by Thomas Field of Bath and standing about 7 ft 9 ins (236 cms). The dotted-minute numbering system on the dial usually indicates it was made later than 1775. Shell inlays to the clock door and base panel are features usually from the end of the eighteenth century or the start of the next one. A pale stringing-line separates the crossbanding on these later eighteenth-century cases. The swan-neck pediment gives the impression of being superimposed onto a flat top, almost as an afterthought. However, this is an original feature and is found in the West Country perhaps more than elsewhere (though a not dissimilar feature occurs in the Newcastle area at times).

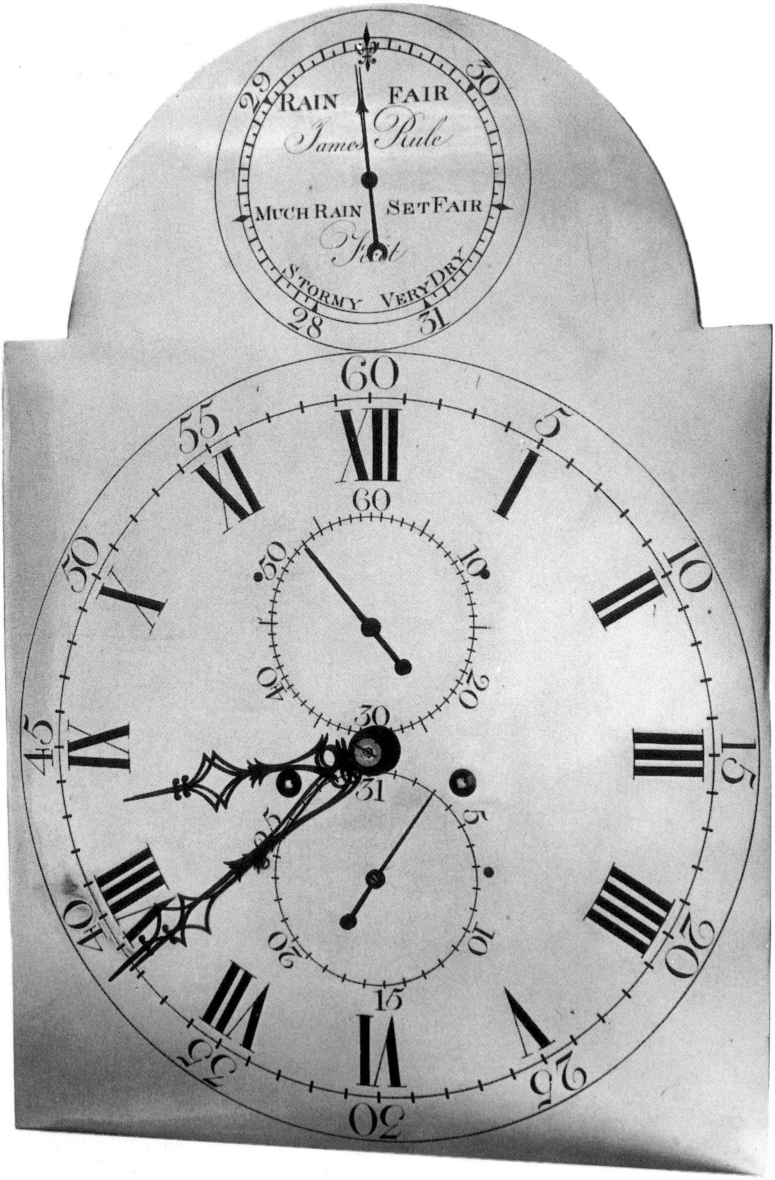

162. Fourteen-inch (38 cms) dial from an eight-day longcase clock made about 1790-1800 by James Rule of York, signed 'James Rule Fecit'. This is a brass dial of the single-sheet type, sometimes called a one-piece dial, whereby all the information is engraved directly on to a solid dial-sheet, and there are no separate spandrels or chapter rings. This type was principally a fashion of the last quarter of the eighteenth century. On this particular dial, dash minutes through a minute line are an almost certain indication of the end of the century. The matching hands are of blued steel, consistent with the date. On this example a barometer fills the arch, an exceptionally unusual feature. With single-sheet dials it was difficult to rivet the dial-feet ends without blemishing the dial-sheet, and sometimes, as here, the dial feet were screwed from the front. The screwheads can be seen beside 50 and 10 on the seconds dial and 25 and 5 on the calendar. Single-sheet dials were usually silvered over the entire surface when new, thus giving a steel-coloured appearance, and these are sometimes mistakenly described as steel dials.

163. Longcase regulator clock made about 1830 by Clare of Preston, with 12-inch (30.5 cms) silvered single-sheet dial, showing separate dial registration for hours and minutes, with centre-seconds hand, maintaining-power and compensated pendulum. A regulator was a clockmaker's own master clock, by which he regulated the timekeeping of his other clocks, though sometimes they might be made to sell to someone requiring extra-precise timekeeping. Most had quite large and imposing cases, such as this; though this case has better proportions and better-quality features than some, for example, the veneer runs up the case in a continuing figure, the feet (front feet only) are gadrooned in pattern, and the base side capitals have nicely carved Corinthian tops. This case stands only 7 ft 7 ins (231 cms) but looks taller by virtue of its relatively small dial. Most have glass trunk doors to allow the compensated pendulum to show. Regulators are mostly non-striking, and have a single train only, as here. They are not quite the same thing as an ordinary domestic clock, and have a specialist appeal to certain collectors.

164. Hood and dial of an eight-day longcase clock with 13-inch (33 cms) dial by Lot Barwise of Cockermouth. This dial has a falseplate marked Osborne & Wilson, which places it in the period of their brief partnership from 1772 to 1777. It is one of the earliest japanned dials. The scenes between moon faces alternate between a starry sky and a landscape – often a sign of an early white dial. The blued steel hands are original. Gold scroll corners have a blue medallion centre. The early form of mouth calendar, as here, is often stopped short with square ends – later ones cover a wider span and have curved ends. The all-mahogany case is of very high quality. The dentil and key-pattern moulds along the swan-necks and below the hood are much finer than most. The blind fretted strip above the trunk door runs round the sides too. The hood door has a gilded quarter bead edging the glass, and rose swan-neck terminals are also gilded. Few brass fittings were used on clocks cases in this area, where wooden alternatives could be applied.

165. This is a very unusual item, indicative of the strength of the fashion change from brass to japanned dials. This is a brass dial (12 ins, 30.5 cms) from a longcase eight-day clock of about 1775-80, which has been japanned over later (probably within twenty years judging by the japanning style) in order to 'modernize' and up-date it. The corner spandrels have been removed, their holes plugged, and the corners painted over with floral sprays typical of a 1790s white dial. The engraved dial-centre has been japanned over in white, with seconds dial and calendar numbers painted on – part can be seen chipped off below XII. The separate chapter ring has had the same treatment, the dotted minute numbering system being the same on brass and on painted dials at this time. There are many places called Salem in the West Riding of Yorkshire, and it is not known which Hardaker was the maker of this clock.

166. A good simple 12-inch (30.5 cms) dial from a thirty-hour clock by Thomas Hargraves of Settle, which could date from anywhere between about 1775 and 1790, probably in the earlier part of that period. The single flowerspray corner is typical, though not all have the extra flowers seen here in the dial-centre, which makes this dial a little more attractive than many. The blued steel hands are original and of non-matching pattern – the straight minute hand also suggests the earlier part of this period. Five-minute numbering with dotted minutes is typical of all dials of this time. The movement is the conventional plated thirty-hour movement of the day. It would be very unusual for a northern clock to have a posted movement as late as this, though some southern clocks still had them.

167. Twelve-inch (30.5 cms) arched dial of an eight-day clock from the beginning of the white dial period. The first known white dials were advertised by Osborne & Wilson of Birmingham in 1772. The raised decoration in the corners and the arch are of gold, imitative of the spandrels of a brass-dial clock. This gold-corner option was available until the end of the century, but the heavily raised type of gold cornerwork seen here is indicative of the very earliest part of this period, roughly 1772-80. This dial is seen in restored condition. The blued steel hands are all original – generally speaking the straight minute hand precedes the serpentine one in time. Many white dials in this period had a mouth type of calendar, but those from later in the century often have larger mouths. Maker William Waren of Thirsk.

168. Simple oak country case of the Waren clock (167), in very sound condition, and not much over 7 ft high (213 cms). Such a simple case would vary little from that of a thirty-hour clock of this period, though this is an eight-day. A simple case with a swan-neck pediment would often have only a single finial, here a brass spire, but sometimes an eagle. A northern clock of this time tends to have a slightly higher base, and therefore slightly shorter trunk, than a similar clock from the south. The oak is quarter-cut, a method of sawing which caused the flecking to show, known as medullary rays. Quarter-cutting was a more wasteful method, but was done because timber cut that way was less prone to warping and made better broad panels.

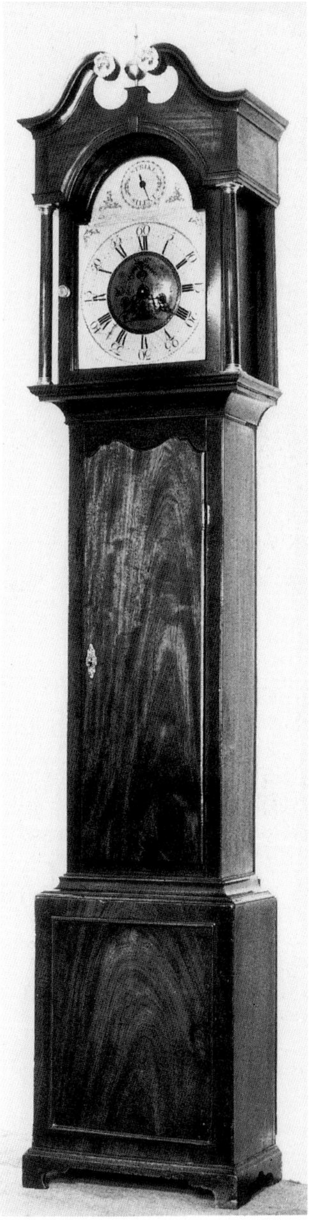

170. Eight-day longcase clock with dial of true enamel, made in the 1780s by W. & C. Nicholas of Birmingham, clockmakers and dialmakers. Such dials were largely experimental as the areas were too large for this form of enamelling. Here the dial-centre (of copper) is a separate section from the surround, and the arch is also a separate piece joined on. Enamel was prone to cracking both in the firing and in later use, as witness certain cracks on this dial. The numbering pattern (5,10,15 minutes numbered and marked by dots) remained consistent from the time of the first white dials in the early 1770s until the end of the century, and the numbering pattern is an immediate recognition feature for a white dial of this first period. The blued steel hands are original, as is the strike/silent lever. The decoration is in pink. The dial-centre is, of course, engraved. Dial 12 ins wide (30.5 cms).

169. All-mahogany case of the clock by W. & C. Nicholas of Birmingham (170). It stands about 7 ft 6 ins (229 cms), and is a relatively simple case with no strong regional features. True enamel dials on longcase clocks are very rare, simply because the process was not a success with such a large dial, and it is doubtful whether much more than half a dozen examples are documented.

171. A very handsome eight-day japanned dial (or white dial as they were originally called) made about 1780-90 for Rowland Griffith of Llanrwst, North Wales. This is a twelve-inch (30.5 cms) dial seen in unrestored condition with original hands in blued steel. The dial corners are pink flowers and are typical of many dials of this period, but the birds in the centre are an extra feature and far less common. These japanned dials were made 'in imitation of enamel' as the original makers claimed. This particular dial was made by Ashwin & Co. of Birmingham, one of the few dial-makers working in the eighteenth century. The craze marks show clearly, though when cleaned and properly restored they would be far less obvious.

172. The rear of the Rowland Griffith dial (171) showing the iron falseplate or backplate impressed with the name 'Ashwin & Co'. Falseplates were sold with the dial. The falseplate feet could be positioned anywhere as required to avoid fouling any part of the movement, so would therefore suit the existing layout of almost any clockmaker. The two holes in the falseplates are there to allow for projecting parts of the movement. The disc of the mouth calendar can be seen clearly, and these are also stamped with the dialmaker's name on some dials. Four pins hold the four dial feet to the falseplate; four falseplate feet hold it all to the movement.

174. Twelve-inch (30.5 cms) square dial of an eight-day longcase clock of about 1790 made by Thomas Long of Stroud, the dial by James Wilson of Birmingham. This is a typical dial of the early Wilson style. The main hands are original of the matching diamond pattern in blued steel, though the minute hand is a most unusual variant having its diamond theme in mid-stem. The seconds hand could be a later replacement. The full mouth calendar is here seen in its complete shape, unlike the earlier shortened version. Note the neatly ring-turned hand collet. This numbering configuration is very easily identified and holds good for almost all the first white-dial period, together with the dotted minutes feature.

173. The case of the Thomas Long of Stroud clock (174), is made entirely of oak and stands 6 ft 8 ins (204 cms). This is a very simple cottage style of case, little changed from a similar type of thirty years earlier. The long door is the most obvious dating characteristic. The hood pillars are free-standing; some southern cases would be more likely to have integral pillars attached to the hood door. The flat-topped door is a feature indicative of the south, for any northern clock of this period would almost always have a shaped doortop. The flat hood top is a feature of many such clocks, necessitated by low ceilings.

175. Handsome eighteenth-century dial with moon-work from an eight-day longcase clock of about 1785 by Major Scholfield of Manchester. The dial is a high quality one, 13 inches wide (33 cms) made by James Wilson, a Birmingham dial-maker. The blued steel hands are original. The seconds hand is in brass as a deliberate contrast and is also original. The two flower sprays in the dial-centre are an extra and are not found on most dials. This type of dial with pink corner decoration is often known as a 'strawberry-corner' dial. Some, like this one, do have strawberries in the corners, but the term is used to describe this general style of eighteenth century dial with double numbers and pink floral corners. The two humps behind which the moon passes normally bear transfer representations of global maps, as here. The maps are often very worn, and these have been restored.

176. All-mahogany case of the clock of about 1785 by Major Scholfield of Manchester (175), standing about 7 ft 10 ins (238 cms). Some cases of this period, especially in this area, have the heavy proportions often associated with Victorian clocks, but in many respects they differ from Victorian examples. Although the door is not as long as on examples with shorter base style, it still fills the whole of the trunk area. Reeded hood pillars do not occur on Victorian clocks, nor do these triple-cluster column forms of the trunk quarter-columns (sometimes known as Chippendale sticks). The triple-pointed Gothic door sometimes occurs on Victorian clocks, but not with this type of surrounding astragal beading. The busy mouldings between trunk and base are much finer than Victorian mouldings, as is the quality of the case as a whole. Book-matched veneers fill trunk and base. The area between the swan-necks is completely filled in on some of these north-western cases, giving a heavy appearance to the hood top.

177. Twelve-inch (30.5 cms) round dial from a thirty-hour longcase clock of about 1780-90 by John Holmes of Cheadle, Cheshire. Some such dials are simply plain white, but here the bird and flower spray adds more colour and interest. The blued steel hands are original. Even without the corner decoration offered as guidance by a square or arched dial, a round dial can easily be dated by the distinctive numbering pattern. Roman hours and Arabic minutes typify virtually all eighteenth-century examples. The mouth calendar here is of the full size, typical of most white dials of the later eighteenth century. Jno. was often used as an abbreviation for John (not Jonathan), even occasionally Ino, as I and J were often interchangeable in script of this period. Note that the hands are held by a screw rather than a pin; screw-fitting hands were not uncommon on thirty-hour clocks in the north at this time.

178. Eight-day white dial longcase clock of about 1780-90 made by Robert Fuller of Watton, Norfolk. The dial is 14 ins wide (38 cms), unusually wide for this period. The dial maker is not named, hence unidentified. The main hands are of blued steel and are believed original. The seconds hand is of brass, but may also be original, as the seconds (and calendar) hands were sometimes made of metals different to the time hands so that they could be distinguished more easily. The gold scrollwork corner decorations are reminiscent of the brass spandrels on contemporary brass-dial clocks, and this type of corner is almost always a feature of an early (Period One: 1770-1800) dial – though not all early dials are of this type. In the arch is a rolling moon, here showing the twenty-seventh lunar day. The configuration of dotted minutes and five-minute numbering is an unmistakable early feature. Most dials of this type are likely to be 12 ins (30.5 cms) wide.

179. The case of the Fuller of Watton clock (178) of *c.* 1780-90 stands 7 ft 10 ins (238 cms) high including its original spire finial. The case is of oak with mahogany inlay in the fan-like decoration to the door top. The unusual cresting to the hood is a variation of 'whale's tail' cresting, a popular East Anglian feature. This one has rather more piercings than some. Wavy back splats to the hood match the wavy top pieces of the hood sides. The mould above the hood door carries an inlay of alternate light and dark diamond shapes in mahogany and holly. Inlaid diamonds in this position are a feature mostly limited to clockcases from East Anglia. The two projections each side of the hood top which look like finial support blocks, are in fact complete in themselves, and the clock never had side finials. The arched-top shape to the trunk door was often used on arched-dial clocks, as it echoes the arch of the dial. It is not particularly a regional feature.

181. An exceptionally fine example of a thirty-hour clock made about 1790 by Lawrence Shakeshaft of Preston, 12-inch (30.5 cms) dial. The bird and flower centre is a nice extra touch. The matching hands of blued steel are original and of foliate diamond pattern – matching pattern hands begin towards the end of the century. The minute hand has a counterbalanced tail to help avoid drag when the hand is rising. The case hood has an architectural pediment and is lavishly inlaid with mahogany alternating with a paler wood (holly?) for striking effect. Half-round pillars at the back of the hood sit against full back splats, an uncommon treatment, though sometimes found in the north-west.

180. The full case of the Shakeshaft clock in oak (181) with considerable trim in mahogany, and stringing and inlay work in alternate dark and light woods. The case is thought to be the work of the cabinetmakers, Gillows of Lancaster, as it has certain features associated with their work. However, no known example of a Gillow case is 'signed'. The height is about 7 ft 4 ins (223 cms). Thirty-hour clocks are often thought of as the poor relation of eight-day clocks, but this case contradicts that view in no uncertain terms. The rounded door top is a feature of many Gillow cases, though others sometimes used this shape too. Note the marquetry panels of inlay below the trunk quarter-columns.

182. Dial from an eight-day longcase clock of about 1790 by Edward Bell of Uttoxeter, typical of the Wilson style of dial. Very few dial-makers worked in the eighteenth century, and the best-known was James Wilson of Birmingham, whose name is sometimes used to describe this general style. The hands are of blued steel and are original throughout. It will be noted here that the seconds and calendar hands match each other, but are quite different from the non-matching main hands. This was often deliberate practice, and is not necessarily an indication of replacement hands. The dial is seen in restored condition, cleaned and with the lettering re-touched. The numbering and lettering was done in a very thin paint, and often survives in a worn state where previous owners have tried to wipe the dial clean, usually erasing part of the numbering. The Deacon dial (195) shows the typical result of amateur cleaning. Unless the services of an expert restorer are available, a dial is best left untouched.

183. The oak case, trimmed with mahogany, from the clock by Edward Bell of Uttoxeter (182). The unusual bracket foot is old, but may be a replacement. The swan-neck pediment was the most common form of hood top on an arched dial clock after about 1750 in areas outside London, especially in the northern half of Britain. This case stands about 7 ft 6 ins (229 cms). In this example the dark mahogany crossbanding contrasts strongly with the paler oak, though the photograph does exaggerate this feature; it is much more noticeable on some clocks than others, presumably deliberately.

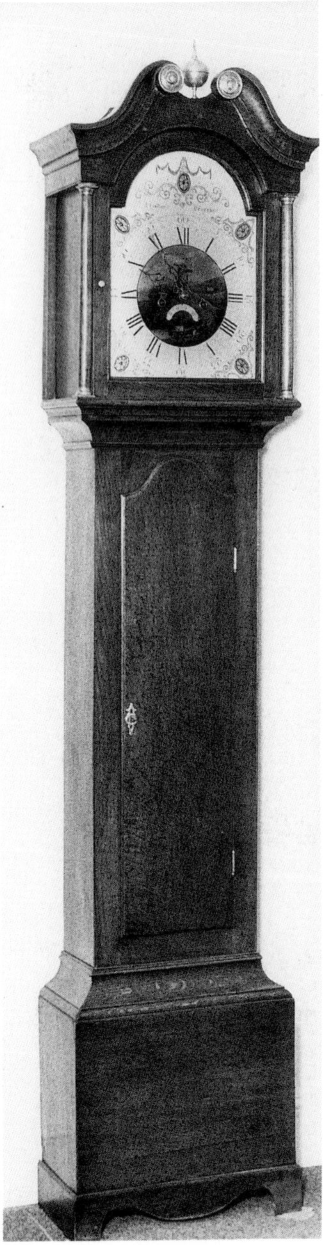

185. Twelve-inch (30.5 cms) white dial from an eight-day longcase clock of about 1790 by James Foster of Peterborough. The decoration in the corners and arch are centred round a shell motif and are of a geometric nature, a feature increasingly common towards the end of the century. The numbering pattern is a clear indication that the date is still within the eighteenth century. The minute hand, though an eighteenth-century one, is apparently an incorrect replacement, as the hour hand is of a style which would have had a matching minute-hand partner. The dial centre is unusual in being painted in the form of a landscape incorporating a windmill. The windmill sails turn as the clock ticks, which looks very impressive but is simply achieved as the sail pipe plugs on to the normal seconds hand arbor, so that the sail jerks on once a second just as a seconds hand would have done. An automated dial of this nature is very uncommon and makes the clock of more interest to the collector.

184. The simple oak case of the James Foster clock (185) is of small stature (under 7 ft, 213 cms) and of slender proportions. Its appeal lies in its simplicity and good condition as well as its small size, for smaller clocks are always in bigger demand today since they can be accommodated in any house. There is little in the way of regional styling in this case and it could have come from almost any part of the country, though it is believed to be the original case for the clock and was no doubt locally made.

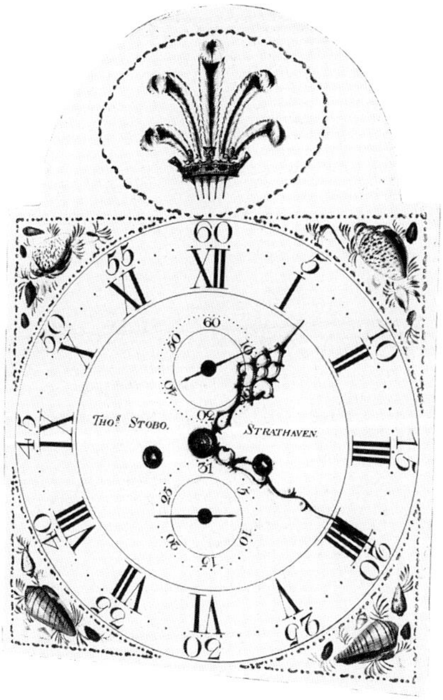

186. Thirteen-inch (33 cms) dial of an eight-day longcase clock dating from about 1790 by Thomas Stobo of Strathaven in Lanarkshire. The corner decoration of sea-shells was popular at this time, as was the 'Prince of Wales Feathers' feature. This is believed to have been first introduced as a decorative feature in 1788 by Hepplewhite, and often appears on clock dials. The hands are of blued steel and are original throughout. This is believed to be a Scottish-made dial – it is considerably thinner than a Birmingham-made dial and capable of being flexed, and the quality of artistry is not as good as a Wilson dial, for example. The dial is not marked with any maker's identification and fixes direct to the movement without a falseplate, whereas most Birmingham eight-day dials of the day have falseplate fixing. The dial is seen here in restored condition.

187. Pine case of the eight-day clock of about 1790 by Thomas Stobo of Strathaven (186). This is unusually small standing only 6 ft 2 ins (188 cms). It was originally painted, as pine cases almost always were, and is seen here in stripped condition, which is the present-day fashion. Side windows to the hood were fitted on many Scottish clocks. The flat door top is often found on some styles of Scottish cases, though seldom in northern England. All the mouldings are of simple form, as pine did not lend itself well to elaborate shaping. The only decorative aspect is the dentil moulding in the hood topmould (sometimes known as dog-tooth moulding). Pine varies considerably in its resistance to woodworm attack. The type which this is, with the heavy and darker grain figuring, is known by some as pitch pine, and seems more resistant than some.

188. Sixteen-inch (42 cms) 24-hour dial of a most unusual longcase clock made about 1790 by John Bolton of Chester-le-Street. The hour hand bears a sun emblem, this giving the effect of the sun passing round the sky, though the clock runs to mean time not solar time. The very long minute hand is counterbalanced to reduce drag. The sky band rotates with its fixed moon face, the moon passing behind a shadow plate to give visual moon phases. The lunar date is shown on the outer arch pointer, the inner one showing the calendar date. The hands on this arch dial resemble a pair of clock hands, and turn independent of each other. The huge disc in the dial-centre bears place-names scattered around the world to act as a world time dial. If used in England, the country where the time is required is set against the sun disc and the time in that country is read off against the word 'England'. The age can be assessed by its conventional features – minute numbering with dots against Roman hours, allegorical corner paintings representing Science, Literature, etc. This clock is a thirty-hour pull-wind; as it probably had to be because a key could not be inserted through rotating discs.

189. Twelve-inch (30.5 cms) dial from an eight-day longcase clock of about 1790-1800 by John Barron of Aberdeen. This is almost certainly a Scottish-made dial, but modelled along the lines of an English dial of the day by Wilson of Birmingham. It has the same type of strawberry corners, but they are of different execution and lack the gold dot-dash borders of the Wilson dial. The arch panel for the name is thrown oddly out of balance by the low position of the lettering, yet this is original. The matching hands are of blued steel and are believed original, they are in what is sometimes known as the curved diamond pattern. The dial has no falseplate fitting and no maker's identification markings, but that applies to some English-made dials as well as some Scottish-made ones. The dial-sheet itself is thinner and more flexible than most English ones.

190. Fourteen-inch (38 cms) dial of an eight-day longcase clock of about 1790-1800 by Joseph Potts of Golborne, Lancashire. This is a dial of the all-gold corner type, yet obviously later than those at the start of this period, the scrollwork being based on an obvious flower centre. Dotted minutes with 5, 10, 15 numbering place this clearly within Period One (1770-1800). This clock also has a centre calendar feature, more popular in the north-west than elsewhere. The hands are original throughout, non-matching steel for the time, brass for the calendar for easy distinction. This dial is large for the period, larger dials often being a preference of the north-west of England ahead of other areas. The scenes on the moon disc in between moon faces are often, as here a landscape alternating with a seascape; a galleon is a more obvious historical scene than a landscape.

191. The case of the Joseph Potts of Golborne clock (190), *c.* 1790-1800. This is entirely in mahogany with bookmatched veneers to the door and base and fan inlays to the base corners, shell inlays below the reeded quarter-columns. These inlays were most popular at the turn of the century. The infill below the swan necks is what is sometimes known as 'verre églomisé', being glass panels painted on the rear (usually blue or green) and painted with gold tracery on the front. These glass infills were mostly confined to Lancashire and Cheshire and are a regional style. The case stands about 7 ft 10 ins (238 cms). The proportions are stocky by virtue of the large dial, and the fact that this case and many of its type have no narrowing to the waist, giving a straight-up-and-down look to the overall balance. The tiny ogee bracket feet are original, though they seem exceptionally small for such a large case.

192. Eight-day white-dial longcase clock in mahogany dating from about 1790-1800 by J. & R. Coats of Wigan. This is a 13-inch (33 cms) dial which gives the case a slightly broad balance. Original non-matching hands are in blued steel. A solid background of colour to the flower corners is usually an indication of the latter part of the century. The case stands about 7 ft 8 ins (234 cms). The turned wooden finials in dark mahogany are original and of a distinctive style, sometimes termed 'Lancashire flying saucer pattern'. The veneers to the door and base are bookmatched and strung round with white lines, probably of boxwood. The ogee bracket feet look disproportionally small but are original. The base has canted corners running to a canted trunk-to-base moulding of a complex nature, typical of the area. These are fine cases and exhibit the finest craftsmanship, though they can appear stocky in proportion.

194. Hood and dial of an eight-day clock of about 1790-1800 by John Wreghit of Patrington, East Yorkshire, here spelt Patterington. This is a 12-inch (30.5 cms) dial with rolling moon. The hands are of blued steel and are believed original. Double numbers (Roman hours with Arabic minutes) together with dotted minutes are a sure indicator of the period. The floral corners here, however, are set into geometric shapes, suggesting a date very close to the end of the century. The case is of oak in a highly distinctive style known as a pagoda, this particular version being limited to this area of north-east England. It would once have had three finials, now missing. In the front of the pagoda top is an inlaid marquetry motif – some have pierced sound frets in this position. The pagoda-hood style is the same in principle as on some London cases, but the execution is different, and it is not difficult to tell an East Yorkshire pagoda case from a London pagoda one.

193. The full case of the clock by John Wreghit of Patrington (194), *c.* 1790-1800. This case is of oak, though grander examples in mahogany were also made. Variations on this type of East Riding pagoda case were made from about 1780 to about 1830. Some have door-top shapes which are quite distinctive, as this example does. This case stands only about 7 ft 3 ins (221 cms), the oak examples usually being considerably shorter than mahogany ones. Many of the oak ones have canted trunk corners, as here.

195. Dial of a thirty-hour clock, seen here in unrestored condition, from a clock by Samuel Deacon of Barton, Leicestershire, a well-known maker, and one capable of outstanding work, though this is one of his standard clocks. The hands are original, but the bluing has been polished away and they show here as bright steel. Both hours and minutes, though still numbered at five intervals and with dotted minutes, are marked by Arabic numerals, a style known as double Arabics. This numbering system was used for only a short period from roughly 1795 to 1805. In this instance we know the exact date the clock was sold by Deacon (1803), as his hand-written receipt dated 22 July 1803 is pasted inside the door, a very rare record. The receipt reads 'Bot. of S. Deacon a clock & case for Mr. Bray, best face, both: £4.10.0. Settled S. Deacon'. The dial was made by James Wilson of Birmingham, one of the better-known dial-makers of this time, and it is referred to in the receipt as 'best face', meaning best quality. The dot-dash borders to the flower corners were painted in gold on a gesso base, so these are raised to the touch. Crazing always shows up more obviously on a dirty dial.

196. Oak case crossbanded in mahogany from the thirty-hour clock by Samuel Deacon of Barton (195). The hood has an unusual architectural pediment with pierced fretwork beneath the topmould. An inlaid flower in an oval panel in the door centre is typical of the kind of decoration found in the doors and base panels of many clocks around the turn of the eighteenth century. The case stands about 7 ft 2 ins (219 cms). The case balance and proportion are typical of many clocks of this time, but the fretted top pediment is an unusual variation.

197. Twelve-inch (30.5 cms) square dial from an eight-day longcase clock by D. Eggert of Temple Cloud, a village in Somerset. The dial is photographed in exceptionally dirty condition, but could be cleaned by a good restorer. The date is about 1805; the dial was made by James Wilson of Birmingham who died in 1809. Here Arabic hours are matched with Arabic minute numbers but only at the quarters – 15, 30, 45, 60 – both being indicators of the early years of the nineteenth century. The corners have scrolls and flowers around central medallions, mostly in gold. A rather unusual extra is the display of fruit within the seconds dial area. The hands are most unusual, being finely made with a flower-petal theme in matching pattern in brass. Daniel Eggert later moved to work in New York.

198. The movement of the eight-day clock of about 1805 by D. Eggert of Temple Cloud (197) showing the dial fixed by its iron falseplate, which is marked for James Wilson of Birmingham but the lettering is hidden in this view. The movement layout is typical of very many, with knopped pillars, the lower ones held to the wooden seatboard by seatboard hooks. The escape wheel and anchor can be seen clearly, and the wheel collets can be seen to match throughout. A non-matching collet on a longcase movement is often a sign of a replaced wheel. Note that the gutline is here trapped over the barrel edge on to the wheel arbor, caused by careless handling.

199. All-mahogany case of the clock by D. Eggert of Temple Cloud, *c.* 1805. This is of relatively simple style and stands only 6 ft 4 ins (192 cms). The flat top to the door is very much a southern feature. The hood door has a wavy edge around the dial, a feature most often found in the West Country. A white string-line of boxwood edges the door and base to break up the uniformity. The door is just developing into the three-quarter length style, with an area above and below it now used for decoration; this indicates the case was made in the early nineteenth century. A swan-neck pediment seldom fits happily on a square dial clock, but here the delicate lines of the swans help avoid a cumbersome heaviness above the dial. Reeded pillars, brass-capped, continue the style of earlier times. Canted trunk corners are mostly a feature of the early nineteenth century, as is the diamond-shaped inlaid boxwood escutcheon for the door lock.

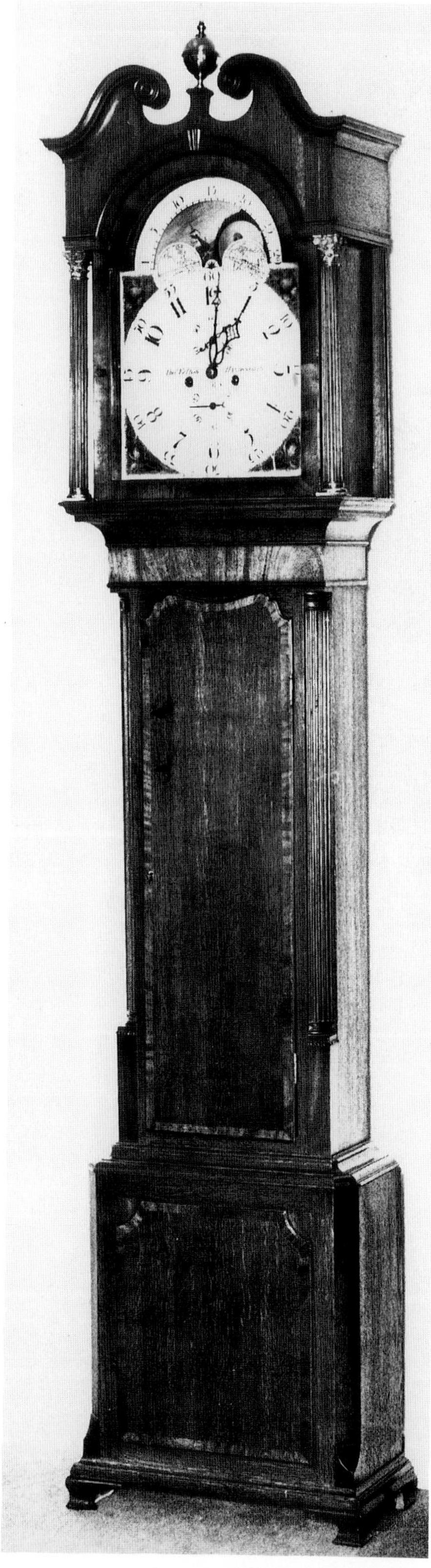

200. Eight-day longcase clock of about 1800-10 by Thomas Felton of Handsworth, Birmingham. The 13-inch dial (33 cms) has double Arabic numbering, matching steel hands and a rolling moon dial. The case is of oak with mahogany crossbanding and stands 7 ft 8 ins (234 cms). The proportion and styling of this case is still of the late eighteenth century with full-length door filling the entire trunk length. The reeded pillars (here with Corinthian brass capitals) and the reeded quarter-pillars to the trunk were common in the eighteenth century but faded from fashion as the nineteenth century progressed. Canted corners to the base and ogee bracket feet are mainly a western and north-western feature.

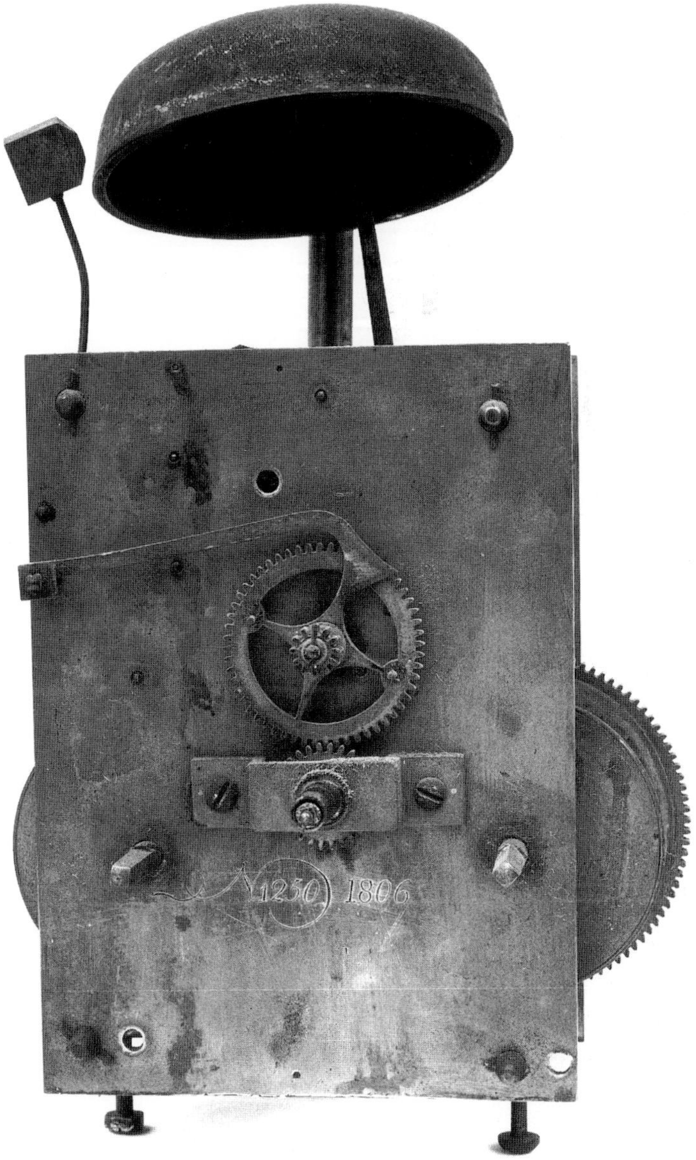

201. View of the movement frontplate in dirty condition from an eight-day clock by Samuel Deacon of Barton, Leicestershire, a highly respected maker who did things in his own inimitable way. Some wheelwork has been removed to show his engraved number 1250 and the year 1806, a feature he put on some but not all of his clocks. This would never be seen except during cleaning. The two bolts below the movement are for fixing the movement to its seatboard by the lower movement pillars. Three empty holes can be seen where the dial feet fit direct, there being no falseplate in this particular example. Deacon regularly made his greatwheels solid, hence no spokes show in the protruding main wheel.

202. Fifteen-inch (40 cms) dial of an eight-day clock of about 1810 by William Nicholas of Birmingham. This dial is larger than most of this period, perhaps to make full use of the painted scene areas. The corners represent the Four Seasons. The dial-centre is fully painted with a rustic scene, an unusual treatment though it does appear on other dials. The two moon 'humps' are also fully painted, again an unusual treatment; the left one represents Justice, the right one Britannia. The matching brass hands are original, brass hands being used increasingly often from now on. Most characteristic of this period is the use of Arabic numbers for the hours and the absence of minute numbers at 5, 10, 20, 25, etc., only the quarter minutes being numbered (15, 30, 45, 60). This numbering pattern is an unmistakable feature of this period. The painting is well done and far superior to the very late stereotyped Four-Season-theme paintings found on some Victorian dials.

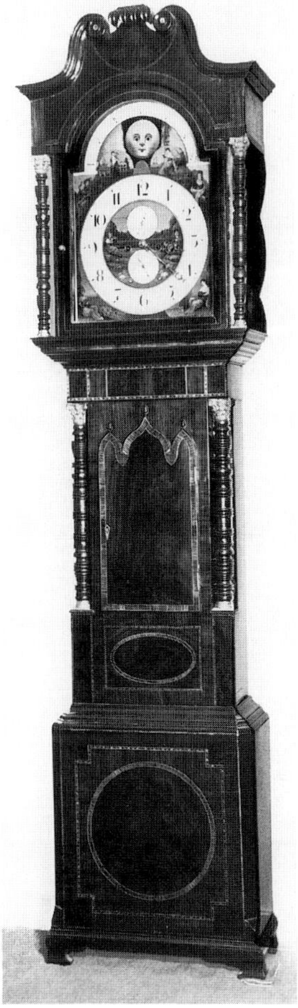

203-4. An interesting comparison of two near-identical mahogany cases. That on the left (203) is the case on the clock by William Nicholas of Birmingham dating from about 1810 (202). It stands 7 ft 9 ins (236 cms), and is lavishly inlaid with crossbanding and stringing of the most ornate form. The triple-pointed Gothic door top was sometimes used much later, and can initially give the case a later appearance than its correct age. The door is short and the space above and below is used for decorative effect. The base features a circular inlaid circle, this circle within a square theme being confined mostly to this period. The right-hand case (204) is from a clock of about 1810 by Edward Garland of Rugby, and is identical in all but a few smaller details, being almost certainly from the same unidentified cabinetmaker. Interestingly, the Garland dial was also painted fully within these extra zones (dial-centre and moon 'humps'). The Garland clock is a three-train playing a chime on the quarter hours. The turned pattern of the hood and trunk pillars are different on each clock. Such turned pillars, especially the full pillars to the trunk, are almost always a Victorian feature, but here their use is earlier and an indication of the very newest style of the day.

205. Twelve-inch (30.5 cms) dial from an eight-day longcase clock of about 1810 by John Smith of Pittenweem, Scotland. This dial was made by James Wilson of Birmingham and illustrates the double Arabic numbering style which lasted only a short time. The matching brass hands are original. Here the moon dial is also a tidal dial, high water being read off from the upright pointer which is variable. A smaller fixed pointer (part broken here) in the arch centre reads off the lunar date. The corner paintings, though still incorporating flowers, a feature of many clocks from Period One (1770-1800), now has a coloured ground and the beginnings of a fan pattern worked into the design, these latter being a distinctive trend of Period Two (1800-30). This dial has a small fly painted on the seconds ring by the 30 numeral. Such dials are known as 'fly dials', the fly usually covers a flaw or chip in the dial surface.

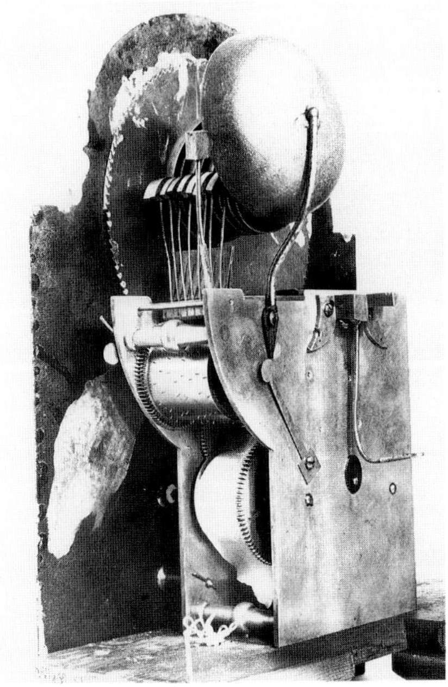

206. The movement of the clock by John Smith of Pittenweem (205), *c.* 1810. This clock chimes the quarter hours on eight bells. The plates can be seen to be of an unusual extended shape to accommodate the chiming train. The nest of bells and the set of hammers can be seen clearly, as can the chiming barrel. The movement pillars are tapered with a knopped centre – pillars are more often tapered on Scottish work than on English. The dial in this example fits direct with no intermediate falseplate, the falseplate was not always used as a fixing method. In this clock the chime and strikework (running from a single train) is positioned on the right; on most clocks strikework is on the left. Note the masking tape round the barrel to hold the gutline from becoming trapped in handling.

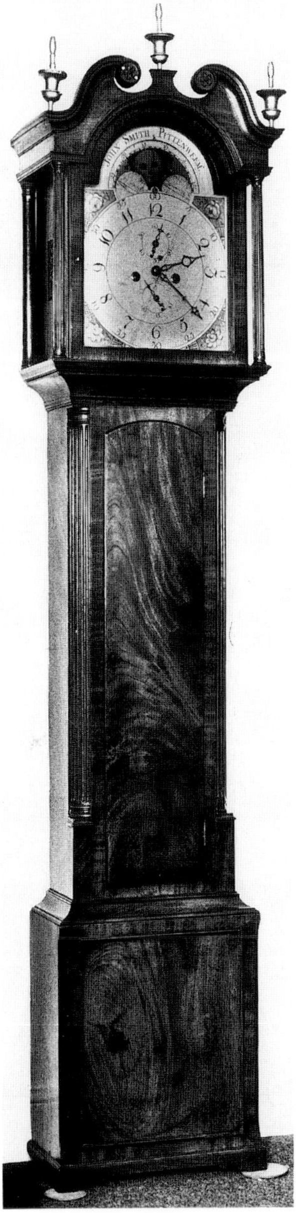

207. The mahogany case of the John Smith of Pittenweem clock (205), dating from about 1810, and standing about 7 ft 6 ins (229 cms). The three flame-pattern (*flambeau*) finials of gilded wood are believed original. Like many cases of this time from eastern Scotland, this case is closely related to contemporary English styles. The swan-necks tend to be small and neat, and side windows in the hood are a feature found on few contemporary provincial English clocks. The shape of the curved door top is a feature found on many Scottish cases of the day and seldom seen on English ones. The styling is restrained, proportions and size being neat and much like those of an English case of a generation earlier.

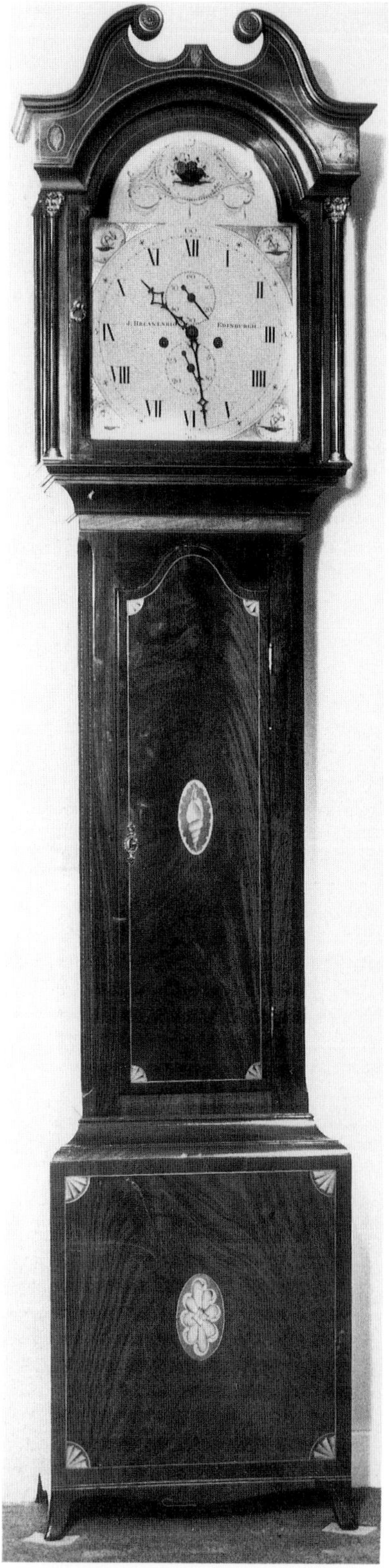

208. Mahogany case of a clock by J. Breakenrigg of Edinburgh, *c*. 1800-10, standing about 7 ft 6 ins (229 cms), the dial 13 ins wide (33 cms). The corners are geometric patterns within which are ships' anchors, a theme of the Napoleonic wars. The numbers are Roman hours with only the quarters numbered in minutes, and a minute line rather than band – all these being features of this period. The case is a good example of the period when the fashion for inlay was popular, especially in the form of fans, roundels and shells. Here each inlay is joined to the next by a white stringing line of boxwood. Note the feet, which are known as French feet and sweep outwards, a feature normally found on clocks only about this time. The hands are of steel and of matching pattern.

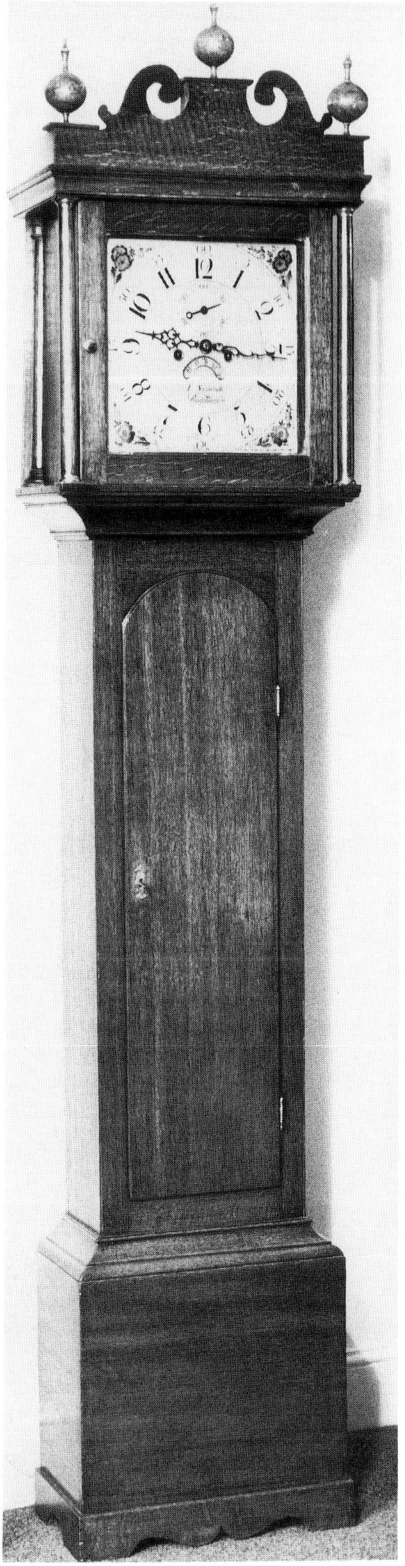

209. Thirty-hour longcase clock of about 1810 by John Spendlove of Thetford, Norfolk. The dial has double Arabic numbers, typical of this period. The case is of oak in a very simple style. The three gilded wooden finials are believed original. The swan-neck is of a style found especially in East Anglia, being of thin oak and having no moulded lip, but cut straight out from thin oak board. This is original, but its simplicity and lack of edge mould often gives the impression that such swan-necks might be replacements. The long door, usually indicative of the eighteenth century, persists in some country casework well into this period. The base on clocks from this area is often, as here, wider than high, and tends to have the grain of the wood horizontal. Northern clocks more often have a high base with the grain running with the longest length.

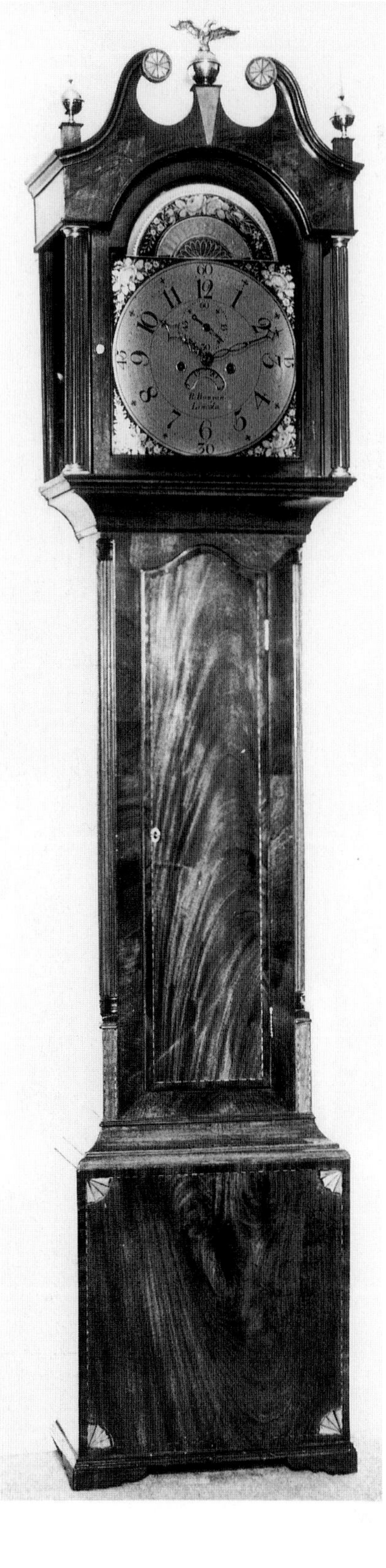

210. Eight-day longcase clock of about 1810-20 by Robert Bunyan of Lincoln. The case is in mahogany, using the finest veneers for the front, and standing about 7 ft 6 ins (229 cms). Fan inlays decorate the base corners, roundel inlays the swan-neck terminals, and chequered stringing breaks up the door and base shapes. The dial is an unusual variation, using tumbling Arabic numbers for hours with minutes marked just on the quarters. The decoration is in gold into a dark ground, and is based on flowers, but much of the arch has become a geometrical pattern. The hands are of a matching pattern in brass. The three brass finials are believed original. The slender and elegant case retains the slimness of line of the eighteenth century and the full-length door.

211. Twelve-inch (30.5 cms) dial from an eight-day longcase clock of about 1815 by John Barnsdale of Burnham, Somerset. A rocking ship occupies the arch, rocking against a backdrop of sea and sky. A tree and castle stand proud at the sides to increase the effect of perspective. Cornucopia in the corners with a little floral trim are indicative of this period when there was a popular taste for shell corners, and shell inlays in the cases. The matching brass hands are believed original. Here the Arabic hour numbers are reversed between 4 and 8 in a manner known as 'tumbling numbers', other examples kept the numbers vertical right round the dial. This inability to settle on a fixed method of presentation for Arabic hours was a feature of the period. Minutes are marked only at the quarters, 15, 30, 45, 60, again an indication of this period. This dial happens to have no calendar, although most clocks did.

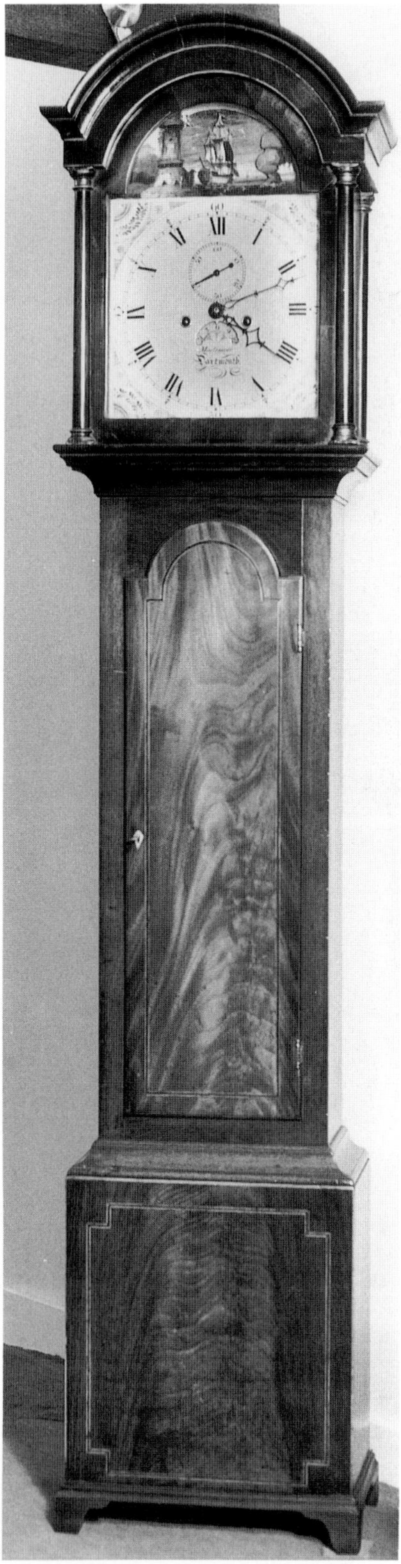

212. All-mahogany longcase eight-day clock by Mortimore of Dartmouth with a rocking ship in the arch. The ship stands proud against a recessed backdrop. The numbering pattern is now in the new Period Three (1830-70) style of Roman hours, with minute numbering running 15, 30, 45, 60 in the manner of Period Two (1800-30). This clock is actually dated 1817. The matching steel hands are believed original. At this time hands might be either brass or steel, but brass became increasingly common. The case stands about 7 ft 2 ins (219 cms). The mahogany is finely chosen for its figure and is decorated by a triple stringing-line inset from the edge of door and base. The door top is of a neutral break-arch style; the dome-topped hood is well-balanced. Pillars are attached to the hood door, a feature lingering in style from earlier times, and a little unusual as late as this.

213. Twelve-inch (30.5 cms) dial from an eight-day longcase clock signed 'John Brown, Wheelwright'. This dial was obviously ordered specially by the (unknown) clockmaker to be lettered with his customer's name, featuring the products of his work and using the tools of his trade instead of numbers. Such dials are unusual, and are an indication of the degree to which each clock was to a greater or lesser degree a bespoke item. Despite the unique decorations for corner and arch, and unique numbering method, it is still possible to identify this dial as from about 1810-1820 by the fact that only quarter hour units are marked in minutes – 15, 30, 45, 60 – a feature only appearing at this period. It is not known who John Brown was. The hands are of matching brass type, but do not match each other. One must be a replacement, probably the hour hand, which looks later in date.

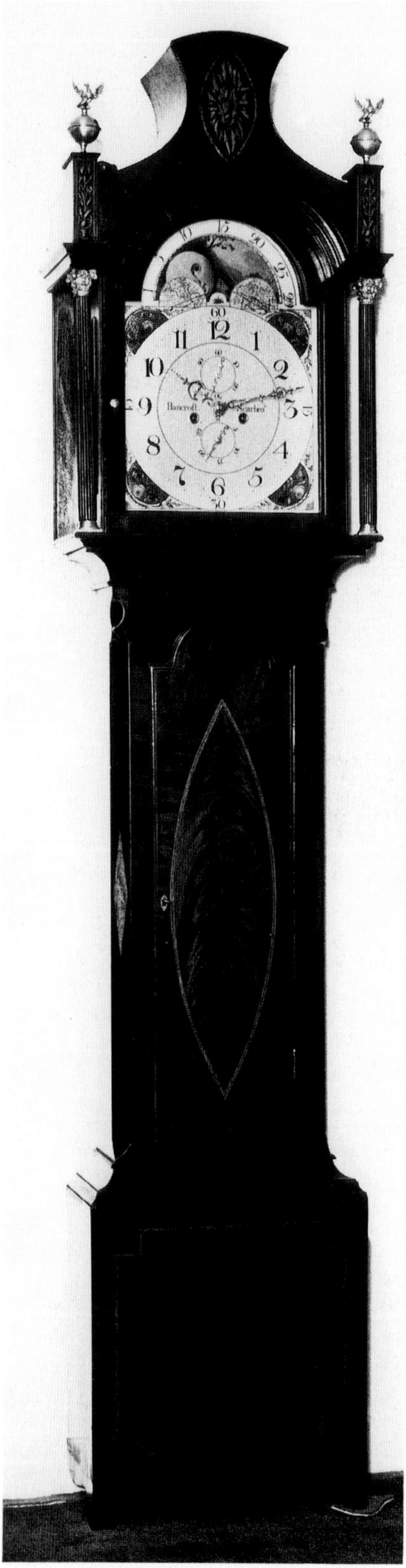

214. Eight-day mahogany clock dating from about 1810-20 by Bancroft of Scarborough. The 13-inch (33 cms) dial shows Arabic hours with only the quarters marked in minutes – 15, 30, 45, 60 – an important dating feature. The case is of the East Riding pagoda style and of very high quality. Much use is made of inlay in the form of marquetry flowers in the finial supports and a large marquetry shell in the hood front. The two eagle finials are original; some clocks have a third in the centre. Many of these cases have an oval panel in the door centre surrounded by radiating veneers in contrasting colour, as here, and many also have a similar treatment to the base section where the panel is square or square with clipped corners. The feet are a continuation of the base itself and are known as semi-French feet. The height is about 7 ft 10 ins (238 cms).

215. Mahogany eight-day clock dating from about 1820 by Samuel McMasters of Ballymena, Northern Ireland. The Arabic hours combined with quarter-hour-only minute marking (15, 30, 45, 60) indicate a date within ten years. The case is of very dark mahogany and has in this instance a plain satinwood oval to the door, where as many other cases have a shell inlay at this time. The door is what is known as a three-quarter door, filling only part of the trunk with a panel below the door to take up what would otherwise be wasted space, and a little inlay above the door for the same reason. The case style has some resemblance to that of north-west England, e.g. the use of wood rather than brass fittings for such items as pillar caps, swan-neck terminals, and lock escutcheon. The swan-necks, on this example at least, stand higher than on most mainland clocks. The height is about 7 ft 3 ins (221 cms).

216. Thirteen-inch (33 cms) dial from a longcase clock of about 1820 by Thomas Mawkes of Belper, Derbyshire. The rolling moon is typical, and there are no particular features by which the clock can be dated. However the numbering pattern has reverted to Roman hour numbers whilst retaining the quarter-minute markers of 15, 30, 45, 60, and this pins it within Period Two (1800-30). The flower corners are unlike Period One (1770-1800) in style, and flowers in varying form can appear at any period. The numbering minute-band is here a single line with notches marked for minutes; single-line minutes appear only in Period Two. The two flower sprays within the dial-centre outside the winding-holes are a carryover from Period One. This dial was photographed during restoration, hence no hands are shown.

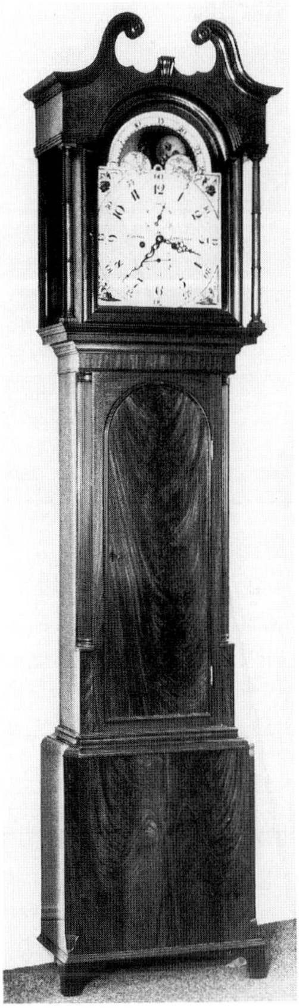

217-18. Two clocks made in Lancaster at different periods are shown together for comparisons. Plate 217 shows a clock by Cawson of Lancaster and dates from about 1800; plate 218 shows a clock by John Jackson of Lancaster and dates from about 1830-40. The age of each is fairly obvious from the change of style in the dials, the numbering changing from double Arabics to single Romans, although the Jackson dial has a black ground, which is unusual at any time, with flowers and highlights in gold. Both cases are believed to have been made by the cabinetmakers Gillows of Lancaster. There are obvious similarities, though the differences are more important as signifying a change of period. The swan-necks are similar, each with the same double curve between the swans, a feature often used by Gillows. The Cawson case has reeded quarter-columns to the trunk; the Jackson has square corners, reeded on the front side – the latter being almost always a nineteenth-century feature. The Cawson pillars are turned in bamboo effect (turn-of-the-century style); the Jackson pillars are more busily turned, a feature of the second quarter of the century. The Jackson has the larger dial, 14 ins (38 cms) against 13 ins (33 cms) – larger generally means later. Thus the Jackson case is broader in proportion, though both are of about the same height at 7 ft 6 ins (229 cms). The mould above the hood door on the Jackson clock is more feeble than that on the Cawson case, which is multi-stepped. The trunks, doors and bases are surprisingly alike, apart from the matter of proportion.

220. Twelve-inch (30.5 cms) dial of an eight-day longcase clock by James Smith of Grantown, Scotland dating from about 1830. The numbering style of Roman hours with no minute numbers is that of the last phase of white-dial clocks, yet the corner and arch decoration is more restrained than later examples. More white ground remains unfilled by paintwork, and the flower themes within geometric patterns are much like late examples from Period Two (1800-30). Most examples of this time and later have the calendar shown by a pointer, as here. The matching brass hands are original, and from now on almost all longcase clocks have hands in matching brass pattern. Most dials of this period are larger than this particular one.

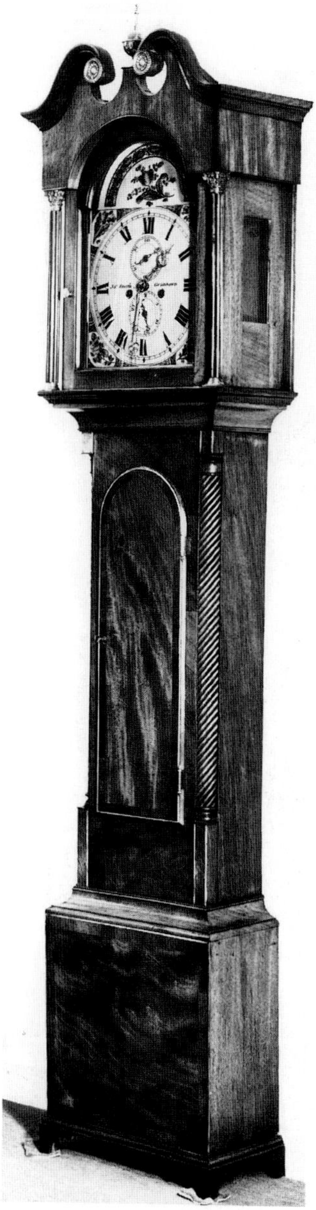

219. The case of the eight-day clock of about 1830 by James Smith of Grantown (220), *c.* 1830. The case is entirely of mahogany with very fine flame veneers to the door and base, the door edged with rosewood banding and finished with a white string-line of boxwood. The overall style and shape is little different from a case of the late eighteenth century, though rope-twist quarter-columns to the trunk are usually a post-1820 feature, and rosewood was seldom used in the eighteenth century. Glass side windows to the hood were popular on some Scottish cases at all periods and do not help in dating. The height is only 7 ft 1½ ins (217 cms), and the dial being unusually small for this period gives a slimness of line more usual in the late eighteenth century. Brass Corinthian capitals to the pillars are a quality feature. The door is a long one, but does not quite fill all the trunk (note the space below it) in the way an earlier one would have.

221. Thirteen-inch (33 cms) dial from a longcase clock of six months duration, *c.* 1830 by Benjamin Greening of Chepstow. The dial is photographed in uncleaned condition. This dial is plainer than some of the period, the arch having no decoration at all, but simply a calendar dial. The hands of blued steel are original throughout, the main hands being unusually slim and the minute hand having a counterbalanced 'tail', all for the purpose of reducing drag, which was especially important with a clock of this nature with a high wheel count – the weights are sixty pounds each! The dial is lettered 'wind up Midsummer & Christmas Day'. The winding of such a clock would become a family event, and this one has a long list of dates of winding penned on its door. The corner flowers are of restrained style, as indeed is the whole dial, but this may be on account of its being a more formal clock than many.

222. The mahogany case of the six-month-duration clock by Benjamin Greening of Chepstow (221), *c.* 1830, stand 8 ft 2 ins (250 cms). Many aspects of its style suggest it was made in Bristol or Bath – or at least in the style of those places. The hood top has a dome topmould above which a curved frill sits between three finial supports, the wavy frill matching the wavy hood back splats. Rope-twist pillars to the hood and trunk tend to indicate a post-1820 date – full pillars to the trunk are usually a late feature. Most of the front is laid out in shaped panels edged in boxwood-lined stringing. The feet are believed original, but are extraordinarily heavy, perhaps on account of the fact that this clock carries 120 pounds of driving weights and would need to be extra sturdy. Many West Country cases of this period are in a similar style.

224. Twelve-inch (30.5 cms) dial of an eight-day longcase clock of about 1830-40 by William Chapman of Lincoln. The matching brass hands are original, with thistle motif centres. On this dial the corner decorations of flower sprays within geometric patterns are suggestive of the beginning of this period rather than later, when full landscape corners became usual. The scene in the arch of the post rider delivering a letter is a printed scene with colour added after printing. Printed dials are uncommon but do occur occasionally. This dial is small for the period. The Gothic-style lettering used in the word 'Lincoln' and the scrollwork tracery around this word are features often found at this time.

223. Oak case, heavily trimmed with mahogany, of the clock of about 1830-40 by William Chapman of Lincoln (224). The height is about 7 ft (213 cms). The small size and slim proportions can sometimes give these cases the appearance of being older than they are. This case has a casemaker's label pasted inside indicating that it was made by Henry Blow of Lincoln. Features which betray the near-Victorian period of this clock are the large areas of mahogany veneer (virtually all the front of the hood) and the three-quarter length door with unused space above and below it. This case would once have had three finials – the upstands can be seen at each edge of the swan-neck and between the swans. The diamond inlay to the door centre seems to have been a favourite with some Lincolnshire casemakers.

225. Thirteen-inch (33 cms) dial of an eight-day longcase clock of about 1830-40 by F. Wood of Bollington, Cheshire. The flower corners are reminiscent of eighteenth-century themes, but are now heavier in style and laid on to a background of solid colour. Two birds to the centre also echo late eighteenth-century styling. However, the numbering pattern of Roman hours without minute numbers is a definitive feature of this period, as is the scrollwork around the lettering. The matching pattern hands are in blued steel, though this pattern is also sometimes found in brass.

226. Eight-day longcase clock of about 1830-40 by J Stokes of Knutsford. The dial has a twelve o'clock moon of the larger, late type, and distinctively numbered Roman hours without minute numbers. Turned hood pillars are a feature of many long cases by this time. The case is entirely of mahogany, as most were by this date. It is very well made with a great deal of boxwood stringing and carefully laid-out crossbanding. The proportions are heavy, partly because of the wide dials of this period – often 13 ins and even 14 (33 cms to 38 cms). The case stands about 7 ft 8 ins (234 cms). Square trunk corners, reeded on the fronts, are typical of the second quarter of the century. The ogee bracket feet, though tiny, are original. The short door is a characteristic of many clocks by this date.

227. Eight-day clock with rolling moon dating from about 1830-40 by Thorpe of Bath. The all-mahogany case is typical of many from this area at this time. This case actually has its casemaker's label inside, a very unusual feature; it was made by William Cock, cabinetmaker of Bristol. The door leaves a considerable area above and below unfilled and hence used for decorative veneering – a late feature. Rope-twist pillars are a late feature too. The flat-topped door is very much a southern style. The swan-neck stands a bit high above the dial, the otherwise blank space there filled with stringing-lines, which can just be seen in the photograph. This high-standing swan-neck is a feature of some West Country cases. The scalloped edge to the hood door is a feature almost always confined to the West Country. Height about 7 ft 9 ins (236 cms).

228. Thirteen-inch (33 cms) dial from an eight-day longcase clock of about 1840 by George Esplin of Wigan. Matching brass hands throughout are typical now; these are believed original. Rustic landscape corners are typical of the time, as are the pheasants (sometimes other birds are featured or hounds and hares, etc). The arch scene is the Garden of Eden, with Adam and Eve as rocking figures. As Eve leans forward to offer him the apple, he leans away to decline. It was a popular theme, though often, as here, the animals were badly painted, not only through poor artistry, but through unfamiliarity with exotic animals. Poor artistry was often less obvious in landscape than in figures.

229. Twelve-inch (30.5 cms) dial from an eight-day clock of about 1840-50 by Pinney of Stamford. Typical Victorian landscapes entirely fill the arch and corners, the paintings even running together around the hour-circle edge. These are clear signs of a dial well into Period Three, even though the dial size is small for this late date. Matching brass hands decorated with surface punchwork are typical of this time. Calendars at this time could be mouth type (as here) or pointer type, the former was cheaper as it required one wheel less to drive it. This dial is in excellent condition, as many late ones are, partly of course because they are much younger than Period One dials (1770-1800), but also because some of these later ones have a high-gloss surface produced by some variation in the japanning process which seems to help them keep their condition.

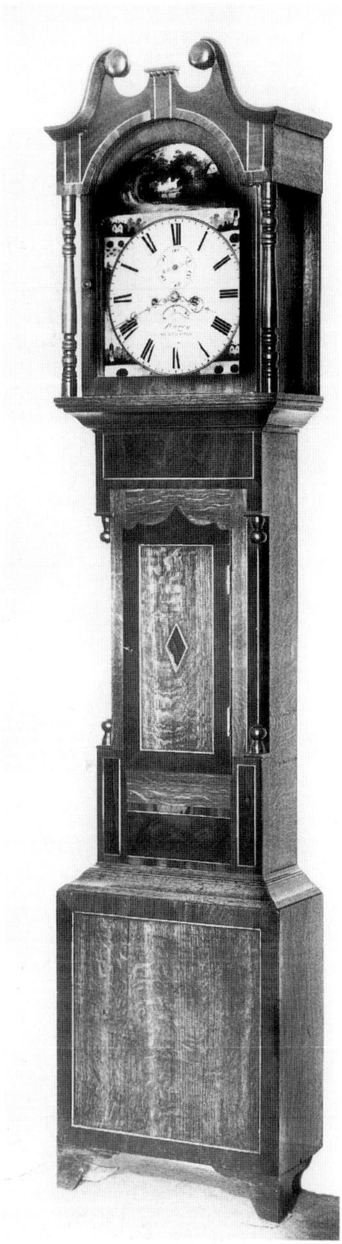

230. Oak-and-mahogany case of the clock of about 1840-50 by Pinney of Stamford (229), standing 6 ft 11 ins (211 cms). Much use is made of mahogany veneer and rosewood as well as white line stringing (in holly or boxwood?). Several features indicate that this clock is Victorian: the short door with considerable 'unused' space above and below it, the turned hood pillars (very different to the round or reeded ones of earlier periods); the turned applied decorative roundels to the canted corners. The extensive use of mahogany trim covering greater areas and in wider banding is also a Victorian trait, although the proportion and size of this clock is relatively restrained, more so than in many Victorian examples. A label inside records the casemaker as J. Wilcox of Dyke.

231. Crudely painted dial of about 1840 from a clock by Richard Snow of Pateley Bridge, Yorkshire. Hunting and shooting subjects were popular at this period, though unfortunately many, like this, were appallingly painted. The appearance of this dial is not improved by the clumsy restoration of the numbers. These dials are colourful, but give every appearance of being painted hurriedly. It was possible to buy a cheap dial at this time for less than half the price of a good one fifty years earlier. The matching brass hands are original throughout, the main hands of a sort of 'crescent moon' pattern popular at this period. Clocks of this time quite often survive with their original hands, which although apparently flimsy, are surprisingly strong.

232. A large dial (15 ins, 40 cms) of an eight-day clock made about 1848-9 by William Murray Junior of Bellingham, Northumberland. This is a most unusual dial showing four hands from the centre – the time in matching brass hands, a long centre seconds hand and a serpentine hand showing the month and date and turning round the dial once a year. The arch is also very unusual, showing a conventional moon dial in the centre, but outside of that a sun disc passes across the sky each day to show times of sunrise and sunset, the horizons raising and lowering to adjust for different seasons. Despite the very unusual layout, the age is easily ascertained by the full Roman hour numbering without minutes and by the landscape corners showing the Four Seasons theme yet again – here better painted than on some examples. As it happens we know to the year when this clock was made, but even without that knowledge the general period is apparent from the style.

233. Thirteen-inch (33 cms) dial from a late Scottish eight-day longcase clock of about 1850-60 by J. Cameron & Son of Kilmarnock. Matching brass hands throughout appear on almost every longcase clock by this time – these are original. All dials of this time have full Roman hour number without any minutes marked. The five paintings (arch and four corners) all run into each other. The arch scene is the 'Cottars' Saturday Night', a well-known scene where the family sit round the table reading the bible; this appears on many Scottish clocks, and in some versions a child sits unnoticed on the floor snipping at the cat's tail with a pair of scissors. The corner paintings represent the Four Seasons. A sort of drapery hangs down to divide the arch from the square part, always a late feature.

234. Eight-day clock of about 1850 or even later by James Davidson of Airdrie. The dial is 13 ins wide (33 cms) and is of the type popular in Scotland illustrating national heroes – Burns, Wallace, Scott, etc. These are Scottish-made dials and often use strong colours with irridescent qualities produced by laying the colour over a silver-leaf ground. This was not a dial style popular in England. The hands are original throughout and are of matching brass. The hood detail shows that this case has no hood pillars, instead multi-angled three-quarter 'pillars' are attached to the door, which is not typical, but more a whim of this particular casemaker. The rounded mouldings to the trunk are a feature of a particular type of Scottish case, and are not found in England.

235. All-mahogany case of the clock by James Davidson of Airdrie (234), *c.* 1850. The convex trunk door is a feature of this case style, the Gothic top-piece above it being attached to the body, not to the door itself. Many of these cases have half-round pillars facing forward to the trunk, as this does, and half-round cushion mouldings above and below the door, as here. This is a very distinctive type of Scottish case, not found in England. The mahogany is often of pale colour but strongly marked in stripes, as this example shows. In this example the feet are missing, they would probably have been small bun feet. The height is less than 7 ft (213 cms).

236. Eight-day longcase clock of about 1850 made by Paul Ganter of Huddersfield. These late Yorkshire cases are often characterized by their bulk with a tiny door, short trunk and massive base. This clock is made entirely of mahogany using excellent veneers very skilfully, but their sheer bulk is against them for today's tastes. The height is close on 8 ft (244 cms). The turned hood pillars on this example are more restrained than many. Turned quarter-pillars to the trunk are almost always a late sign. The raised panel on the base of this example is only one variation on a theme; some have a sunken panel, and some have a flush surface to the base. By this late date almost all longcase clocks are made of mahogany.

237. Thirteen-inch (33 cms) dial from an eight-day longcase clock of about 1850 by R.W. Farquharson of Dundee. The corner themes show the always popular Four Seasons, though the execution here is a little different, and the quality of painting is certainly better than that of many other examples. This dial was photographed during restoration, and is therefore without its movement or hands. The arch scene represents an incident from Walter Scott's poem *The Lady of the Lake* (written in 1810). Many Scottish dials of this period take literary and historical subjects as their theme, often representing some Scottish subject or historical character, real or fictional. The numbering pattern remains static after about 1830, with Roman hour numbers and minutes not numbered at all.

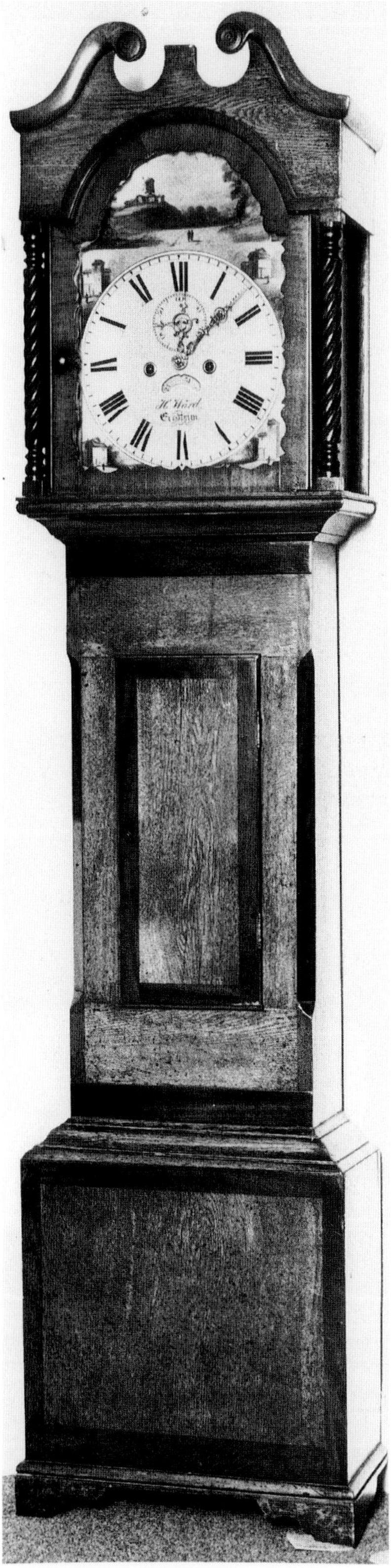

238. Eight-day clock of about 1850-60 made by H. Ward of Evesham. The 13-inch (33 cms) dial is typical of the time with painted ruins and landscapes, and the matching brass hands which all longcase clocks have by this date. The case is of oak with mahogany trim, the short door being indicative of the period. The flat door top is a feature seldom seen in northern clocks, especially at this late date. Rope-twist pillars are a late feature. The height is only about 7 ft (213 cms). The wavy-edged hood door (sometimes called scalloped) is a feature almost exclusively confined to the West Country. The topmould to the swan-neck is really only a flattened quarter-round moulding, rather feeble compared to the multi-shaped top-mould of a better quality case. The oak is mostly straight-sawn and shows little figuring, and the overall effect is rather plain.

3 *Tavern clocks*

Tavern clock is the name usually given to a large weight-driven wall clock designed primarily for use in a public building such as a coaching inn. Examples of this type of clock are known from the early eighteenth century, though surviving examples are few before mid-century. The name often given to these clocks is Act of Parliament Clock, though this is misleading. The act from which the name derives was passed in 1797 and repealed within nine months. Its effect was to impose a tax on watches which almost destroyed the watch industry. The theory was that this tax produced a sudden boost in public clocks of this type, but since many such clocks pre-date the act, a more sensible name by far is tavern clock.

Tavern clocks were large, the dials often being as much as 30 inches in diameter, the height often as much as 6 feet, as they were intended to be clearly legible across a vast room. In principle the movement was much like that of a longcase clock, but almost all were single-train clocks, having no strikework. Most had an additional wheel in the train (five wheels) to give eight-day duration within a drop considerably shorter than that of a longcase. The anchor escapement was that normally used, and as the movement plates contained far less than a conventional eight-day longcase clock, narrower plates were often used, frequently tapered towards the top and known as A-plates from the shape of the letter A.

Most of the earlier examples had dials made of joined wooden planks, painted on the surface. Many had a black background with gold numbering, though some later ones had white grounds with black numbering. The cases of many were japanned or lacquered with a black background and gold highlights in the oriental manner.

Tavern clocks are not common items today. Many must have been scrapped in the past, perhaps after their exposed dials (for they had no glass protective doors) had been re-painted on so many occasions that they were discarded for smarter, newer clocks.

Some later examples had japanned dials of iron, the same kind of dials as a longcase clock. These dials were usually smaller, around 12 inches and the cases were therefore narrower and often shorter. This smaller type is often known as a Norfolk clock, though they are by no means confined to that county. Most surviving full-size tavern clocks were made south of a line from Birmingham to the Wash.

239. Tavern clock of about 1760 in the style known as a 'shield' dial, black with gold numbering and decoration. This example bears the legend 'Tempus Rerum Imperator' (Time rules everything) where many would carry the name of the maker. This was the motto of the Worshipful Company of Clockmakers and was used by many clockmakers, both members and others. The construction can be clearly seen to be of three large vertical planks, typical of the wooden-dial type. The height is about 5 ft (153 cms). The original hands are of brass and the minute hand is counterbalanced to avoid drag. The single weight of such clocks was often brick-shaped, sometimes chamfered at the front to allow full drop within the shaped case base. This clock has a single train, being a timepiece, as almost all were. Shield dials were amongst the earliest tavern clocks, this shape of dial falling into obsollescence by the 1790s. (*Photo: Strike One Ltd.*)

240. Round-dial tavern clock of about 1760 by Thomas Daws of Northampton, typical of many of the period. The decoration and numbering are in gold on black. The brass hands are original with heart-shaped tips, a popular theme, and the minute hand is counterbalanced against drag, as most were. The dial is about 30 ins (80 cms) in diameter and the height is about 5 ft 8 ins (173 cms). The circular dial area joins to the straight-sided trunk by small, shaped 'earpieces', a feature of many such clocks, though some have lost them. The trunk base sweeps back to the wall with an ogee surface, this shape varying considerably between clocks. On many clocks this base section has been replaced or restored on account of damage from falling weights crashing through the base.

241. Tavern clock by John Wright of Dorking, the dial 28¾ inches diameter (73 cms), height 4 ft 10 ins (147 cms), dating from about 1780-90. The wooden dial is white with black numbering. The hands are of brass with heart-shaped tips, the minute hand counterbalanced. The case is japanned with a black ground and gold highlights. The door is decorated with a varnished print (a fashion also found on longcase clocks occasionally). The theme is a well-known one: the young lady picks the pocket of the gentleman she is entertaining, whilst her accomplice looks on round the corner. The movement has tapered plates and four-wheeled, four-pillar movement. The winding-hole has a brass dust cover, as many once did. The earpieces are especially well-shaped. (*Photo: Strike One Ltd.*)

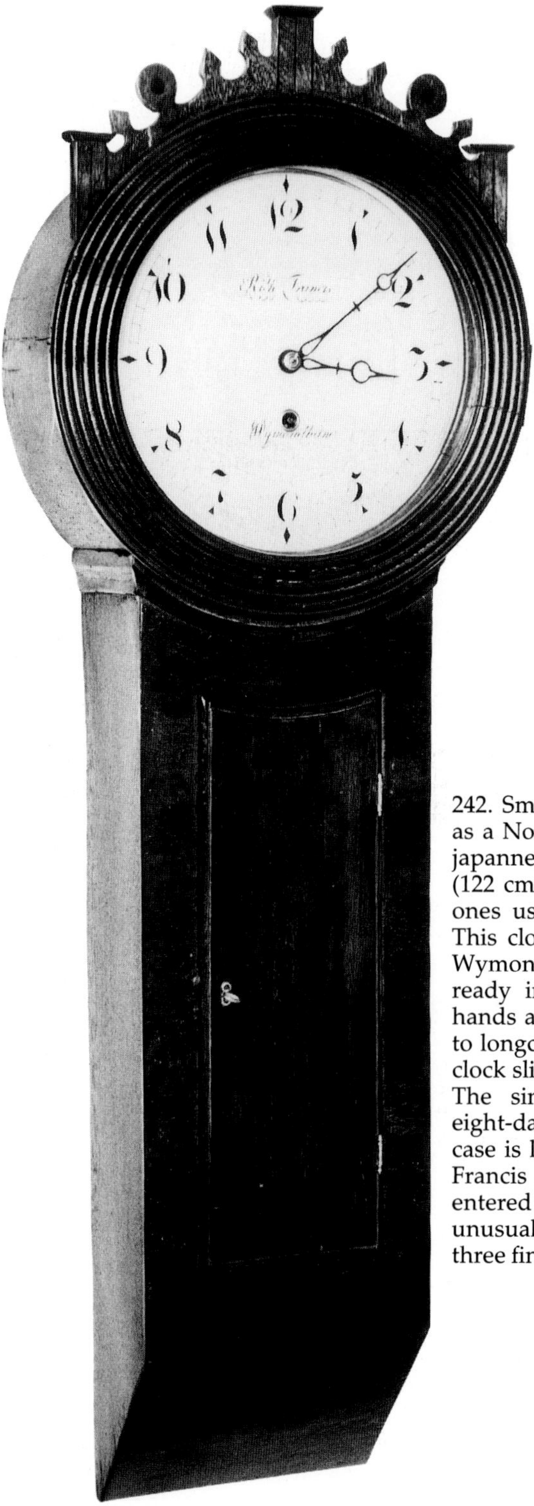

242. Smaller type of tavern clock, sometimes known as a Norfolk clock, this one has a 12-inch (30.5 cms) japanned iron dial. The case is of oak, about 4ft high (122 cms). Unlike larger tavern clocks, these smaller ones usually have an opening glass door, as here. This clock was made in 1812 by Richard Francis of Wymondham, Norfolk. The Arabic numerals are a ready indicator of period on japanned dials. The hands are of matching pattern in blued steel, similar to longcase clock hands of the day. The hood of this clock slides fully off, just like that of a longcase clock. The single-train movement has five wheels for eight-day duration in a short drop. On the back of the case is lettered: 'S.Wright bot. this time piece of Mr Francis Sep 14 1812', which was the day Napoleon entered Moscow. The multi-turreted top fret is unusual but is original. The clock may once have had three finials, like a longcase.

243. Weight-driven wall clock with 13-inch (33 cms) silvered brass dial, made about 1830 by Isaacs of London. The case is in mahogany and is 4 ft 10 ins high (147 cms). The single-train, five-wheel movement runs for eight days. A more formal clock such as this is unlikely to have been used in a tavern, but more probably in a bank or public offices of some kind. Its appearance is similar to a wall regulator, and though this clock does have maintaining-power and a seconds dial (both unusual features on such clocks), it is not a true regulator. Mahogany examples are often known as Norfolk clocks, not a very satisfactory name for clocks such as this example, but there is no generic name which covers each variation adequately. The hands are original and are of matching pattern in blued steel. The Gothic door top and curved gadroon carving below the dial are typical Regency features.

4 *Bracket clocks*

Bracket clock is the name given by collectors to British spring-driven table clocks. Some were intended to be used on a table, especially a bedside table for night-time use, which is why very many have repeating facilities to enable the nearest hour to be established in darkness by a pull-cord. Others might have been used on a mantelpiece. Still others had a wall bracket on which the clock itself would have sat. The great majority never had any bracket of any kind, and many of those that once did have since lost their brackets. But whether they once had a bracket, never had a bracket or still today have one, they are all named by the same term, bracket clocks.

Bracket clocks were powered by springs, the nature of which is to pull strongly when fully wound, and progressively more weakly as they run down. This plays havoc with timekeeping, and the fusee gear was used on virtually all British spring clocks in an attempt to reduce (if not remove) this built-in problem of power loss. A weight-driven clock on the other hand has a constant driving source, and no spring clock will ever equal this integral asset of a weight clock. But there were other problems with springs. The very process of spring-making was to hammer a piece of iron until it was long enough to coil and uncoil repeatedly without breaking. Breakage in use was an even greater problem, when the sudden shock to the wheelwork could cause expensive damage.

Spring clocks were costly to make, imperfect as timekeepers, and delicate in use, a combination of problems aggravated by the far dustier household conditions of the past. For these reasons, spring clocks were always the property of the well-to-do. Before the introduction of the pendulum (1658), all these problems were aggravated by the balance-wheel escapement, which was less than accurate even when weight-driven. A mere handful of spring-driven table clocks survive from before 1600 in this country. More survive in the next half century, but until the coming of the pendulum such clocks were more in the nature of amusing novelties for the very wealthy, than serious household clocks. The vagaries of a change of temperature affected all clocks, especially spring clocks where even the driving power itself (the spring) was subject to expansion and contraction in addition to the wheels and pinions.

Bracket clocks in the later seventeenth century, were made by the select few for the select few. The finest craftsmanship and materials went into the making of these clocks; the quality was more important than the price.

Bracket clocks of the second half of the seventeenth century were often made of ebony, later ones were made of pearwood stained with black polish to resemble the more costly ebony and known as 'ebonized'. By the 1680s walnut examples are known, and sometimes olivewood. In the eighteenth century, bracket clocks sometimes had japanned cases (also known as lacquer). Walnut veneer was popular in the first half of the eighteenth century, sometimes with marquetry inlay, though marquetry was always uncommon. Occasionally tortoiseshell veneer is found. Mahogany took over after about 1760 as the predominant wood, but the ebonized case style lingered on in bracket clocks into the 1790s, perhaps because it was thought that black would show off the brass and silver well, and also because black would fit in with most kinds of decor. Oak was seldom used as a surface wood.

The verge pendulum, or bob pendulum as it is sometimes called, was used in bracket clocks almost until the end of the eighteenth century, long after the anchor escapement was known to have superior timekeeping powers. The anchor escapement required more careful setting into beat, and was less happy about being moved, especially to a surface with a different level. The verge escapement was far less fussy about levels and was provided with a carrying handle (sometimes two) and a carrying hook on the backplate, into which the bob pendulum could be rested during carrying. It could be carried into the bedroom at night and returned to the drawing room at morning without affecting its timekeeping.

The anchor escapement became usual on bracket clocks from about the start of the nineteenth century, and remained common until the end of British clockmaking in about 1850 or 1860, after which time most clocks were imported. However, because of its superior timekeeping, the anchor escapement was often used to replace the verge on some clocks, and many a bracket clock built originally with verge escapement was modified to anchor later in its life. Collectors usually refer to 'original verge' to identify those which have never been changed. Today restorers sometimes re-convert to verge those which have at some time been modified to anchor, and such a clock is described as a 're-converted verge' to distinguish it from an 'original verge'.

Some bracket clocks have a pull-cord, principally for bedside use, to allow the clock to repeat the last hour, or sometimes the nearest hour, using the power of the mainspring of the strike train. Another system, known as 'pull-repeating' did the same thing without drawing power from the mainspring. Pulling the cord wound a separate spring, and releasing it allowed the strike or chime to operate. Pull-repeating often included the quarter-hour chimes and might be as few as one bell or as many as eight, or even more. This is known as 'pull-quarter repeating' and chimes the nearest quarter-hour unit *and* the nearest hour. Pull-repeating is not found on any other type but bracket clocks. Ordinary repeating can occur on longcase clocks too.

244. Ebonized bracket clock *c.* 1680-85 by John Knibb of Oxford, one of England's finest clockmakers. It is signed in the early manner below the chapter ring 'John Knibb Oxon Fecit'. The case stands 12½ ins (31.5 cms) excluding the carrying handle the dial is 6¾ ins square (16 cms). The hands are believed original and are of blued steel. The movement has verge escapement with five latched pillars and four latched dial pillars. The clock has either-side pull-repeating facility, repeating the quarters on one bell plus the hour on the hour-strike bell. The clock has rack striking, here positioned within the movement plates. A strike/silent lever can be seen above XII. The minutes are numbered within the minute ring, as was normal at this period. Many clocks of this type have feet, but this one was made without them, as was normal practice for this maker. (*Photo: Richard Barder Antiques.*)

245. The finely engraved backplate of the John Knibb of Oxford bracket clock (244). At this early period bracket clocks were usually signed on the backplate as well as on the dial. The verge pendulum is seen here in its carrying hook. The decoratively shaped tails of the bell stands can be seen at each side at the top, one being the hour bell, the other the pull-repeating bell. Note the lavish engraving based on tulip themes, all within a plain-lined border. The verge pendulum bob usually had a slim lining of wood into which the pendulum rod screwed, as the wood allowed finer regulation than a metal thread did. (*Photo: Richard Barder Antiques.*)

246. Ebonized bracket clock dating from about 1680-90 with pierced basket top and frontal mounts in brass made by Thomas Cruttenden of York. The maker was trained in London and the style is that of London work. The blued steel hands are believed original and are typical of the period in that they are easily distinguished from each other. Minutes are engraved within the narrow minute band, a feature which changed by the end of the century. Half-hour markers are formed from meeting arrowheads, a sign that the end of the century is approaching. The dial-centre is matted with no engraving at all and no ringing of winding-holes, all features of the period. The four flambeau-style top finials are believed original. Height 14½ ins (39 cms) including carrying handle. Dial 5¾ ins (14 cms). (*Photo: R. Sewell.*)

247. Backplate of the bracket clock by Thomas Cruttenden of York (246) dating about 1680-90. The engraved design is based on tulips, a recurrent theme in the second half of the seventeenth century. The pierced apron holds the pendulum within its V-slot and prevents its arbor moving forwards or backwards. The pear-shaped pendulum bob is typical, the pendulum here being at rest in its carrying hook. At this period many bracket clocks were signed on the backplate as well as on the dial. The design of the engraving attempts in some degree, though not entirely, to encompass the arbor ends within its pattern. For instance, the lower two acorns are centred around the barrel arbors. (*Photo: R. Sewell.*)

248. Bracket clock in tortoiseshell-veneered case, made by William Farrer of Pontefract and dated 1707. The shallow arch is indicative of the early years when the arch was just coming into fashion. The clock is finely decorated with lavish engraving, including the dial corners where cast spandrels would be more usual. The maker was obviously very proud of this clock, putting on the dial the full date of manufacture and the owner's name, Buckley Wilsford. The blued steel hands are believed original. Note the very unusual half-hour marker, which is simply a large dot. Provincial bracket clocks of this great age are very uncommon. Tortoiseshell examples are uncommon anywhere. It is possible the engraving was done by someone other than the maker, as the name is spelt Ferrer, whereas this maker and others of his family usually spelt it Farrer. Height about 15 ins (40 cms).

249. The quality of the engraving can be seen better in this close-up of the dial of the William Farrer clock (248). Gulielmus was Latin for William, and Latinized signatures (and in this instance Latin inscriptions too) give the work a more high-blown formality. By the word 'formavit' the maker means 'created it'. The upper inscription is a phrase capable of more than one meaning: 'It is always wise to have one's fortune in the law. Buckley Wilsford is my rightful owner.' Perhaps Buckley Wilsford was connected with the legal profession.

250. Backplate of the William Farrer bracket clock (248) bearing his signature yet again. The outside countwheel shows clearly, an early feature, as does the verge pendulum with typical pear-shaped bob, here resting on its carrying hook. Signing the backplate of a bracket clock as well as the dial was more usual on early examples, but was gradually discontinued, and by the third quarter of the eighteenth century backplates are normally unsigned. The designs of engraved patterns to backplates are a helpful guide to dating as they change gradually over the years. These changing patterns can only be learned by studying enough examples regularly.

251. Bracket clock in burr walnut, *c*. 1700, made by John Sanderson of Wigton. The height is 15 ins plus handle (40 cms). The clock has pull-quarter repeating on two bells. It can be seen to be a verge escapement clock by the mock pendulum feature across the upper dial-centre on the back of which is engraved the maker's name. At the top of the dial, above 60, the N-S indicates a lever for striking or non-striking setting. At the side of this is engraved 'Memento Mori', a favourite inscription with this maker, meaning 'bear death in mind'. The hands could well be original. Half hours, quarter hours and half-quarters are clearly marked at this period. The matted dial-centre has engraved work only around the calendar box. Engraved corners are an unusual alternative to spandrels on bracket clocks. Herringbone engraving surrounds the dial, less often seen on bracket clocks than on longcases, but a fashion of the day. (*Photo: Aspreys Ltd.*)

252. Dial of a bracket clock of about 1715-20 by John Gerrard of London. The matted-centre carries no engraved decoration, but has the cut-out below XII for the mock pendulum. This is a twin-fusee clock built originally with verge escapement. This can be seen by the dial since the mock pendulum feature only appears on verge clocks. The half-hour and quarter-hour units are marked on the chapter ring at this period, and so in this instance are the half-quarter markers. The spandrel pattern is a type of sphinx head. The arch carries two sub dials; that on the right for strike/silent operation, and that on the left being fine tuning for time regulation (which avoids the need to open the back of the clock for access to the pendulum regulation nut). The engraved work in the arch is especially fine. The hands are of blued steel and are believed original. Dial size 7½ ins wide (19 cms).

253. The backplate of the bracket clock by John Gerrard of London (252) is also signed with his name and is finely engraved. Note the herringbone-engraved border which is repeated on the fastening straps. This clock was built with verge escapement but was converted to anchor later, as many were. The lever above the back cock is for adjustment of fast/slow regulation and acts by raising or lowering the pendulum by means of the lever on the dial. With this particular backplate no attempt has been made to lay out the engraved design around the arbor ends. This tends to be a feature of the earlier periods.

254. Ebonized bracket clock made about 1710 by John Crampton of Dublin, with twin fusee and verge escapement. The pierced frets in the door and case sides are to let out the sound. The clock has pull-repeat facility on three bells. When operated, a pull-repeat will sound one peal of the bells for each quarter hour plus the count of the last hour. Its purpose is believed to have been principally for bedside use at night, when the time could be established to the nearest quarter hour without striking a light. The shape of this case is typical of early bracket clocks, which at this period mostly have square dials. Glass side windows enable the movement to be viewed. Most have a carrying handle, as here, for one great advantage of such a spring clock was that it was portable and could be taken upstairs at night, the verge escapement not being over-sensitive to varying levels of surface. The style of this clock is slightly behind the times and much resembles London work of twenty years earlier. This top shape is known as a basket top.

255. The dial of the John Crampton of Dublin bracket clock (254), *c.* 1710, is 7 ins (17 cms) square. The style of the dial is much like a London dial of twenty years earlier. Tiny minute numbers within the double band, ringed winding-holes, tiny cherub-head spandrels, and a little engraving around the calendar box, could all be seen on a London dial of 1690. Meeting arrowhead half-hour markers, however, are usually a sign that the century has turned. The calendar here happens to be below XII, but was more often above VI, its position being principally a whim of the maker. The nest of three bells for the quarters and the single hour bell can be seen protruding above the dial. The hands are of blued steel and could well be original.

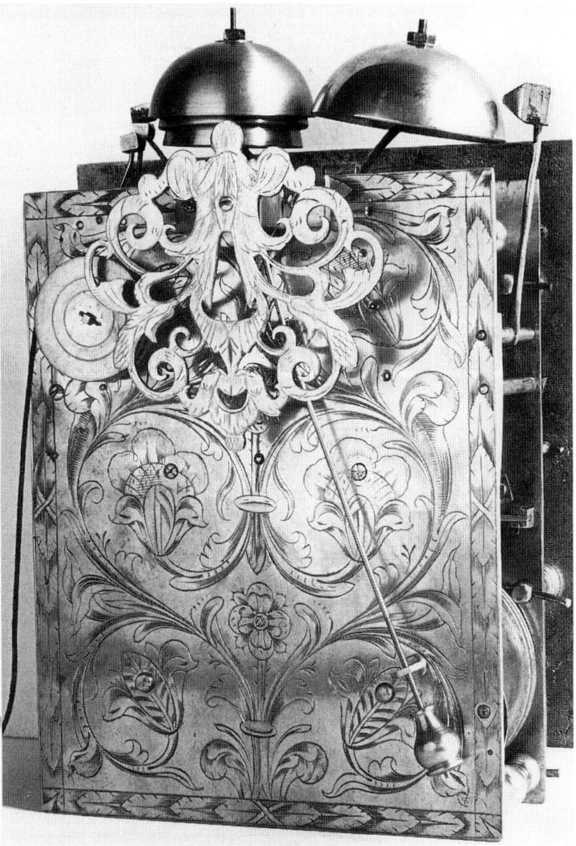

256. Side view of the movement of the bracket clock by John Crampton of Dublin (254), *c.*1710. The fusee of the strike train can be seen with its gutline part wound on to the spring barrel. Note the very unusual pillar shapes of a double baluster instead of the more normal knopped centre pillar – probably a measure of the maker's independence of thought. The centre pillar, however, which can just be seen in the photograph, is of conventional shape, suggesting that the maker put the extra effort into just those pillars which showed. There are five pillars in all. Part of the verge escapement can be seen, in particular the contrate wheel.

257. View of the John Crampton of Dublin bracket clock (254), *c.*1710, from the back, showing the finely engraved backplate of floral nature with a herringbone edging. The engraved apron, which covers the pendulum rest and acts too as a retaining clip, is a replacement, and the engraving on it can be seen to be of a lesser quality. The pendulum is here seen at rest in its carrying hook. The pull-repeat pulley (and the barrel which contains its spring) can be seen upper left with its pull-cord attached. The back of the dial sheet can be seen to be in its raw state with casting marks and blemishes. This is normal as the filing and planishing work with which all major parts were finished was very time consuming, and was not carried out on parts such as the dial back, which were not on view and did not need hardening as they carried no moving parts.

258. Ebonized bracket clock made about 1715-20 by Joseph Antram of London, 'Watch & Clock maker to his Majesty' (George I) as he announces on both the dial and the backplate. This is a timepiece only with alarm work and stands about 15 ins (40 cms) high. This shape of top is sometimes known as a bell top. The dial is typical of the period with matted-centre, half- and quarter-hour units marked on the chapter ring, and original blued steel hands. In the arch is the alarm setting disc, here set to ring at 5 o'clock. The clock has pull-repeating on two bells to sound the nearest quarter hour. The alarm work is also operated by a pull-load system, with its own independent pulley and spring barrel so that it does not draw power from the mainspring. The ornate carrying handle is original.

259. View of the backplate of the Joseph Antram bracket clock (258), *c.* 1715-20, showing the superb engraving, the two loading pulleys for alarm work and pull-repeating, and the engraved straps for holding the movement firmly in its case. The verge pendulum is here seen at rest in its carrying hook, the pear-shaped bob being typical. The ornate movement pillars (two showing here) are knopped at the centre with incised rings for decoration and raised flanges, typical of such early work – this type of pillar is sometimes known as a ringed pillar or a finned pillar. The two bells are for the repeating system, chiming ting-tang quarters when operated. The larger bell is also used for the alarm, being rung by a double-headed hammer on its inside. Fine workmanship by a Royal clockmaker.

260. View of the movement of a double-fusee (two-train) bracket clock with verge escapement made about 1725 by Barnaby Dammant of Colchester. The spring barrels can be seen well, as can the fusees, the contrate wheel and verge (escape) wheel. The bob pendulum is seen resting in its carrying hook, which most verge clocks had. The engraved backplate just shows with its herringbone edging. The movement has five pillars with knopped centres and decorative turned rings, and is typical in many respects of any verge bracket clock of the period – even at later periods the layout barely changed. Behind the top of the arched dial can be seen the cam for strike/silent operation.

261. Bracket clock with lacquer decoration in black, the clock made about 1730 by Thomas Utting of Yarmouth. The chapter ring marks half hours with a small diamond and quarter hours are also calibrated on the inner chapter ring. A calendar feature fills the arch, below which is a strike or silent lever. The mock pendulum showing below XII indicates that the clock was originally built with verge pendulum. This is a two-train double fusee movement, but it also has pull-repeating work on six bells. A pull-repeat system is self-loading when used and does not draw power from the clock's springs. This chimes a peal of six at quarter past, two at half past and so on. The blued steel hands are believed original, as is the brass carrying handle. Total height about 20 ins (50 cms).

262. Backplate of the clock by Thomas Utting of Yarmouth (261) showing the ornate engraving typical of the period, *c.* 1730. Note how the pattern is designed to incorporate the protruding pivots of the arbors. The fastening strap on the right can be seen to be original with its engraved herringbone edging, whilst the left-hand one is plain and a later replacement. The six bells and hammers can be seen top left beside the pull-repeat trigger – a spring loads the power on pulling and releases it when the cord is released, thus it does not draw power from the clock mainspring. The clock was built with verge pendulum and later converted to anchor, as many were. Thus this pendulum is a replacement and the back cock from which it hangs is not engraved to match the backplate.

263. Ebonized bracket clock made about 1730-40 by Joseph White of London, of standard height (about 22 ins, 56 cms) including handle. This is a three-train (triple fusee) clock chiming the quarter hours on six bells, the power being supplied by the third train. The winding-holes are laid out symmetrically in an original three-train clock. Strike or silent in the arch was commonplate, especially on chiming clocks. The blued steel hands are probably original. Half- and quarter-hour units are still calibrated on the inner chapter ring at this time. The slot below XII shows the mock pendulum, which indicates that this clock was made with verge pendulum. The signature appears on a curved nameplate. No engraved decoration appears on this matted-centre.

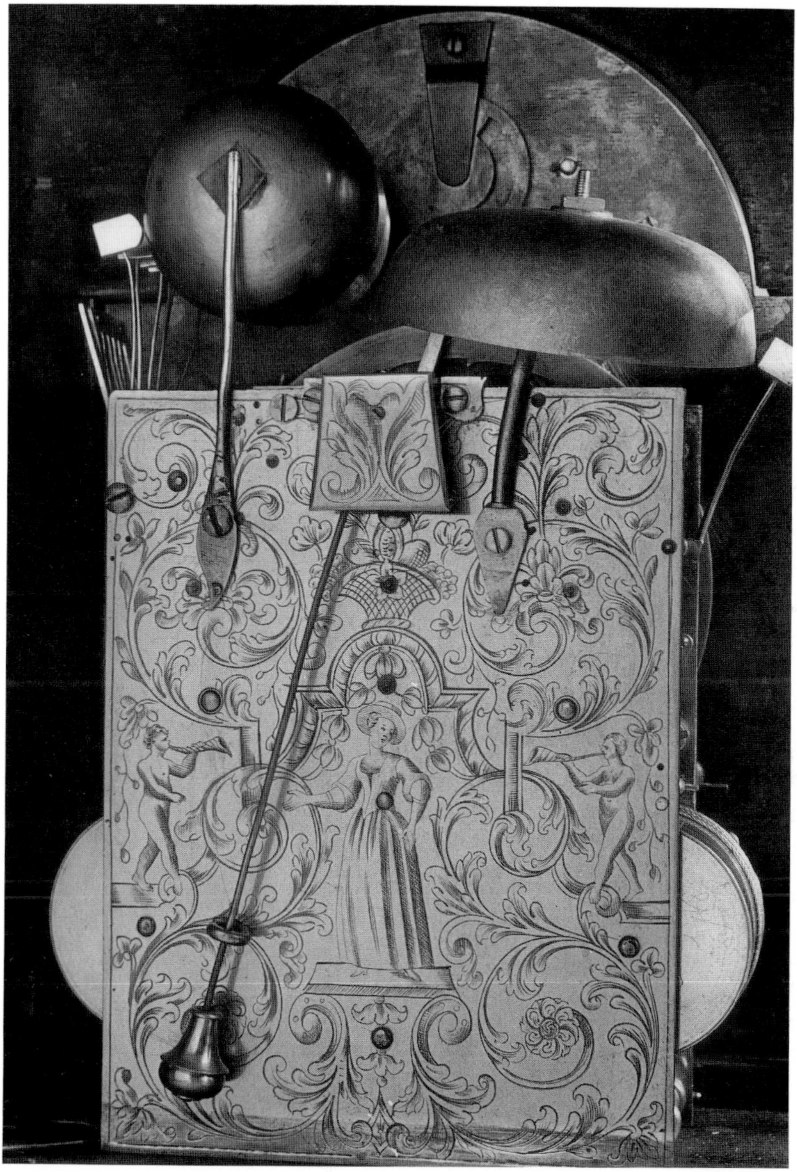

264. View of the backplate of the bracket clock by Joseph White of London, *c.* 1730-40. This has its original verge escapement with typical pear-shaped bob, the pendulum here seen resting in its carrying hook, with which such clocks were normally provided. The 'apron' covering the supported end of the pendulum acts as a restraint so that it cannot be shaken out of its resting point in moving. This is a finely engraved design, though the engraver has not tried to work the pivot ends into his overall pattern but has largely ignored them, although some (e.g. the rose in the centre of the flower basket) have been incorporated. This engraving is characteristic of this period, in its subject matter and the treatment of the scrollwork, being very different from backplate engraving later in the century. With practice one can almost date such a clock from the engraving pattern alone.

265. Ebonized bracket clock of about 1760-70 by John Green of London. This is a slightly larger clock than some, standing about 24 ins (61 cms). The carrying handle and flame-type (flambeau) top finials are original. The applied carvings around and above the door glass are unusual and are gilded, as are similar ones around the side windows, not visible in the photograph. The engraving, typically by this time, shows Chippendale-period styling – scrolls and temples, etc. This is a double fusee clock. The strike can be switched off by the strike/silent lever in the arch. The hands could well be original, as by now the serpentine minute hand was fashionable. The hands are of blued steel.

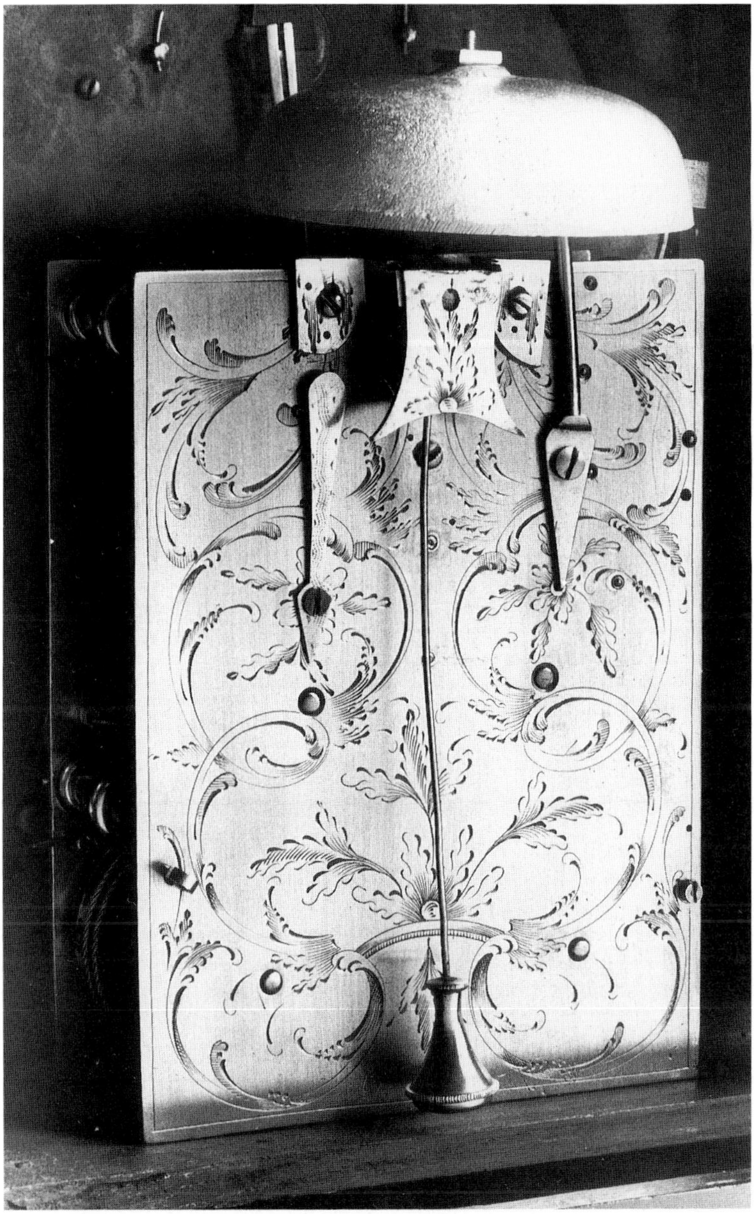

266. Backplate of the clock by John Green of London (265), *c.* 1760-70, pictured with the clock inside its case. Here the verge pendulum is seen hanging at rest; the unused carrying hook is on the left. The engraving is of high quality, though no attempt has been made to incorporate the pivots into the design. The engraving is not exactly a mirror-image based on the centre, but each side is balanced against the other. This movement has no side straps to attach it to the case. Instead it is held by bolts through the lower pillars from under the seatboard, rather like many longcase clocks. Behind the dial arch can be seen the turnplate for the strike/silent switch.

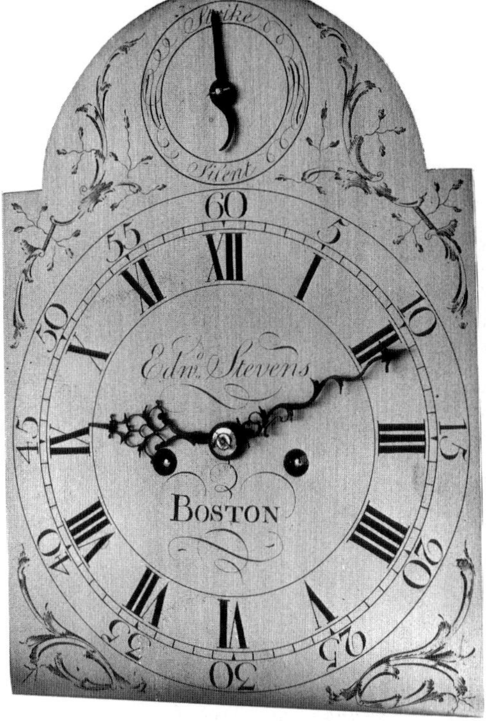

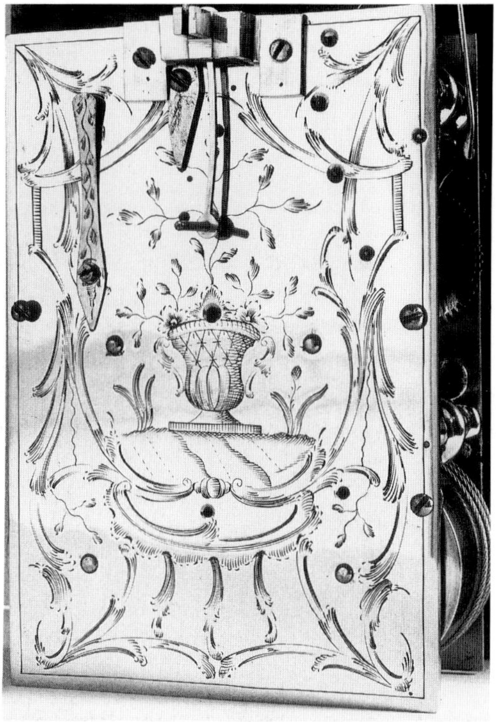

267. Double-fusee bracket clock dating from about 1770 and made by Edward Stevens of Boston, Lincolnshire. The blued steel hands are original. This dial is of the single-sheet type, silvered all over. On these dials engraved work is normal instead of spandrels, chapter ring, etc. The engraving represents twigs and branches in the Chippendale style, with a strike/silent switch in the arch. The dial is about 7 ins (17 cms) wide. By the time this single-sheet dial style was fashionable, the marking of half-hour and quarter-hour units had long ceased. Earlier single-sheet dials, as here, mark minutes by a continuous double band; later ones use the dotted minute system. There is no clue from the dial of such a clock as to whether its escapement is verge or anchor; this one was in fact built with a verge.

268. View of the backplate of the bracket clock by Edward Stevens of Boston (267), *c.* 1770. The engraving style of branchlets is typical of the Chippendale period. The pendulum back cock, from which the pendulum hangs, is a replacement, fitted when the clock was converted from verge escapement to anchor. This single-point crutch happens to be an alternative to the usual system, where the pendulum sits within a fork. The engraved bladespring on the upper left is for power to shunt the strike/silent work back and forth in and out of gear. Note the heavily knopped movement pillars just visible to the right of the backplate.

269. Double-fusee bracket clock with single-sheet silvered brass dial made about 1780 by Thomas Moss of Frodsham. The dial is very finely engraved with scrollwork, the design balanced around the winding-holes, for example. The use of dotted minutes (as on a contemporary white dial) is an indicator of age. The blued steel hands are original, though of slightly unusual form. A rolling moon is a little unusual on a bracket clock and more likely to occur on a provincial one than on one from London – moonlight was far more important in the country for night travel. The case is of red walnut and of unsophisticated style. The bracket feet are original and resemble small versions of ogee bracket feet on longcase clocks from the area, being most unusual on bracket clocks. The height is about 15 ins (40 cms). Wooden sound frets on the case sides are unusual on bracket clocks, again being smaller versions of longcase clock hood frets. Many features of this case suggest that it was made by an experienced maker of long cases who was unaccustomed to bracket clocks.

270. Mahogany-cased bracket clock made about 1790 by Thomas Lister, Junior of Halifax, standing about 20 ins including the carrying handle (50 cms). Fan inlays decorate the case corners, joined by boxwood stringing-lines. Inlays such as fan patterns are a feature of the end of the century; they were made of a variety of woods such as holly, and often burnt to produce a shading effect before polishing. This is a double-fusee clock of the single-sheet type of silvered brass dial. The four corner finials are replacements, but the handle is original.

271. Dial of the bracket clock by Thomas Lister Junior of Halifax (270), *c.* 1790. The single-sheet silvered dial is 7¾ ins wide (19.5 cms). The engraving work is especially fine, particularly the hatching which shades the darker areas. In the centre of the arch is a calendar feature, to the right of which is a strike/silent dial, and to its left a faster/slower regulation dial. The blued steel hands are original throughout. The minutes are marked by dots, a feature of the latter part of the century. The engraved work shows lingering traces of Chippendale style, but the hanging flower swags suggest a stronger Sheraton influence. Excellent work by a highly skilled maker.

272. View looking down into the escapement of the Thomas Lister bracket clock of about 1790 (270). The escapement is a form of anchor but runs on a pin-wheel rather than a normal toothed wheel, and this is known as a pin-wheel escapement. It is occasionally found on bracket clocks but is unusual at any time. The chiming barrel can be seen to the right as this clock chimes ting-tang quarters on three bells – here the large bell hides the smaller two, and two of the three hammers are removed.

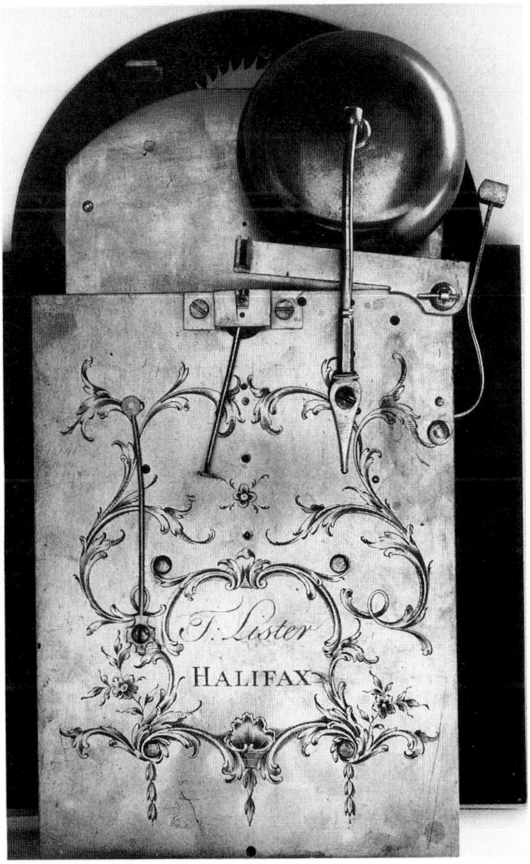

273. View of the backplate of the Thomas Lister bracket clock of about 1790 (270). This is signed again on the backplate, a practice of some makers, which had been largely discontinued by the early nineteenth century. The engraving is of late Chippendale influence, working some of the arbor pivots into the design. Note the exceptional steelwork in the crafting of the bell stand, which is multi-faceted in three dimensions. The movement frontplate is extended upwards to support the rear-of-dial work for the subdials – calendar, strike/silent, and fast/slow regulation.

274. Mahogany bracket clock, the front inlaid with box-wood stringing-lines, made in 1819 by Fulton Combe Gerrans of Wortley, Gloucestershire. The clock stands about 16 ins (42 cms) and the convex white dial is 8 ins (20 cms) in diameter. The brass carrying handles and fishscale side grilles are original, as are the ball feet of brass. The dial style marks minutes in units of five, slightly old-fashioned for this date. The glass door opens for access to the hands, but this one is unusual in opening leftwards. The hands are of blued steel and are original, in a style sometimes known as teardrop. The movement is a twin fusee with anchor escapement.

275. Backplate of the bracket clock by Fulton Combe Gerrans of Wortley (274), 'near Wotton under Edge', dated 1819. The bell has been removed for the photograph to reveal a very ornately engraved backplate in which every care has been taken to incorporate pivot ends, etc., into the design. It is unusual for a backplate to be engraved as late as this, and very rarely is any backplate dated as well as signed. Every attached item, including the fastening straps, has been shaped finely into a teardrop purely out of pride of workmanship; each item would have functioned equally well if left plain. The making of such a clock would be an infrequent event for a rural clockmaker, which is no doubt why he went to such lengths to record his name and the date. Such interesting work can sometimes be found in what at first sight appears to be a very ordinary bracket clock.

276. Frontplate of the bracket clock of 1819 by F.C. Gerrans of Wortley (274), seen here with the dial removed. The layout is conventional, except that this clock has a starwheel-and-jumper system behind the snail, a feature sometimes fitted to a clock to ensure accurate repeating facility. The repeater trip arm itself has been removed. Note again the teardrop endings to some of the attached parts, including even the rack spring and jumper spring, indications of good craftsmanship. Shaped shoulders to the plates are another nice touch – plain squares would have done equally well in terms of function. Note that two score lines on the left-hand setting-up click match with two on the plate itself by the right-hand click – an indication that some restorer has put each back in its incorrect place!

277. Double-fusee bracket clock of about 1800-10 made by Braithwaite and Jones of London. The case is of rosewood inlaid with brass stringing-lines, with the original brass carrying handles, fish-scale side grilles, and brass ball feet. The dial is of the japanned type in a full arch. The hands are of blued steel and could well be original, though they do not 'match' as most of this period do. The height is about 15 ins (40 cms). Note how the door lock is skilfully concealed, its keyhole hidden within a brass clover-leaf inlay. Rosewood was very popular at this time and was often combined with brass inlay work. Anchor escapement.

278. Double-fusee bracket clock of about 1810-20 by Frodsham of Gracechurch Street, London. This is a larger clock standing about 22 ins high (56 cms). The case is of mahogany with brass inlay, mostly in the form of stringing-lines. The pineapple finial is original as are the brass fish-scale side grilles and brass ball feet. The dial is a full-arch-type japanned dial with strike/silent option in the arch. The hands are original and are made of brass. Note the keyhole is concealed within a brass inlaid flower head. Anchor escapement.

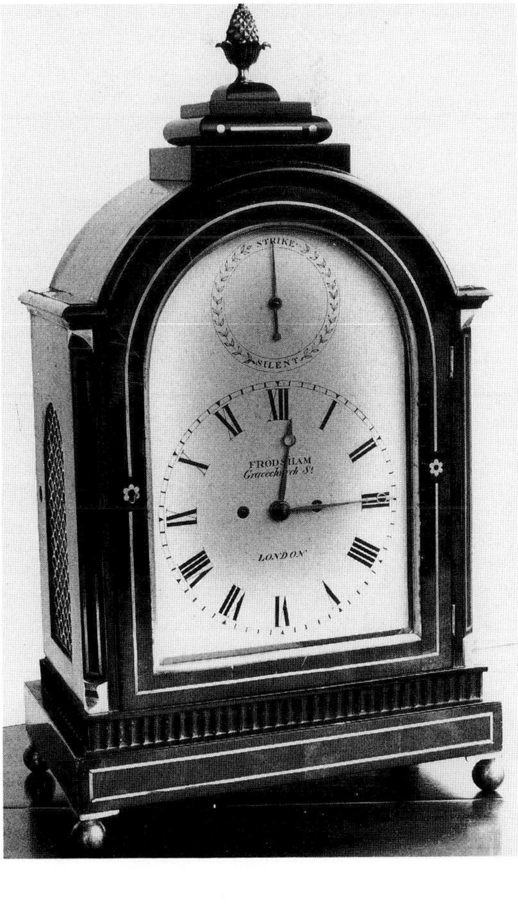

279. Back view of the bracket clock by Frodsham of Gracechurch Street, London (278), *c.* 1810-20. The movement can be seen to rest on a seatboard and also to have its two retaining bars. The anchor escapement pendulum is here seen at rest, held by its carrying screw. Note that the backplate is stepped and has clipped corners, just for stylish effect. The maker's name and address are engraved on to the backplate, though by this date decorative engraving on the backplate had generally fallen out of fashion. Note that the work is finely finished – back cock, pendulum restraint and bell stand all have neatly shaped teardrop ends, which have no function beyond good appearance. The strike barrel can be seen protruding beyond the plates on the lower right and carries a chain rather than gutline. Chain drive is always regarded as a plus pointer on a fusee clock.

280. Very grand and imposing bracket clock in the Egyptian style which came in with the Napoleonic wars. This clock dates from about 1810-20 and stands 19 ins (48.5 cms) with a 7-inch (17 cms) convex dial. The matching hands are original in blued steel, and are of the crescent moon pattern common at this period. The case is in mahogany, with much use of brass inlay and brass sphinx figures to the corners. The chamfer top is gadrooned and has its original pineapple finial. Brass side grilles are of the Gothic type to let the sound out. The movement has twin fusees and anchor escapement. The gadrooned bracket feet are original. Note the finely decorated brass bezel to the glass door – most are plain. Altogether quite an 'important' clock.

281. Double-fusee bracket clock of a particular style known as a Lancet Top, or just a Lancet, characterized by the pointed Gothic top shape, *c.* 1810-20. This clock stands about 17 ins (43 cms). The maker is James Ferris of Poole, Dorset. Brass side grilles and side carrying handles, as well as brass bun feet, were a feature of most Lancet clocks. This one however has the additional feature of a brass pillar and bead framing the front corners, and by no means all have this. The inlay work to the front of the mahogany case is typical in its geometrical style. Some cases have the inlay in brass; others such as this one are inlaid with light wood, probably boxwood. The hands are original and are made of blued steel.

282. Bracket timepiece (i.e. non-striking clock) made about 1830 by Lewis Abrahams, Junior, of St James's, London. The clock has an 8-inch (20 cms) circular brass dial with silvered surface and stands 19 ins high (48.5 cms). The clock is veneered in rosewood and inlaid with brass decoration, mostly in the form of stringing-lines. The blued steel hands are original, and of matching crescent-moon pattern. The carved decorative top-piece is still of a restrained nature; later (Victorian) styling was more ornate. Brass side grilles are of a vaguely Gothic nature, as they often are at this time. The bun feet are original. The movement has anchor escapement with single fusee movement. Rosewood was used particularly in Regency times, and very little outside that period. By this time minutes have long since ceased to be numbered on the dial, which is marked with hours only.

283. Ebonized bracket clock, showing much use of brass inlay, made about 1830 by T. Hammond of Manchester, with twin fusee and anchor escapement. The height is about 15 in (40 cms). The chamfer top is gadrooned. The brass side grilles are of the fish-scale pattern. The side carrying handles are original. A repeater cord can be seen just in front of the carrying handle, a feature believed to have been most used during darkness by a bedside which allowed the clock repeat the nearest hour. The dial is a white (japanned) one. The blued steel hands are original, of teardrop shape, common at the period. This is a handsome clock, its brass inlay showing particularly clearly against the ebonized background.

284. Mahogany bracket clock (strictly speaking a timepiece, i.e. non-striking) made about 1840 by Taylor of London. This is quite a small clock standing only 15 ins (40 cms) with a 6-inch (15 cms) white dial. The dial is convex, as many were at this time. The carved front to the top of the clock is more ornate than in earlier periods. The front of the case is veneered in finely figured mahogany, whilst the sides, which are less visible, are in plain solid wood. The movement is built with single fusee and anchor escapement, which was the kind of escapement almost all bracket clocks had from now on. The brass ring carrying handles at the sides are original, though they look a bit large for a clock of this small size. The matching hands are of blued steel and are original in simple, ace-of-spades style, common to many bracket and wall clocks of this time.

285. View of the work behind the dial of a bracket clock of about 1840 by King of Loughborough. This is a two-train clock chiming ting-tang quarter hours on two bells, which is achieved by having four steps (counting the top lip) of each hourly position on the snail. The rack and rack tail show clearly. Note the unusual baluster shapes of the movement pillars, stepped shoulders and 'feet' to the plates, large-headed screws to hold the plate to the pillars instead of the usual taper pins. Note also the decorative and fancy shapings to e.g. the spring click ends, the rack, the rack hook, etc. These are purely for decoration and done as an indication of the maker's pride in his work. All this is never seen by the owner of such a clock, unless he happens to see it during cleaning by a restorer.

286. Double fusee bracket clock in mahogany with brass inlay made about 1840-50 by George Lee of Skipton. Height about 20 ins (50 cms). Brass inlay work was popular in the 1830s and 1840s. Here the white dial is of an unusual shape, no doubt chosen because of the eccentric pattern of the case which shows a Chinese pagoda influence. The dial decoration is in twisted gold strapwork. Many bracket clocks of this time have brass side grilles, here of a Gothic pattern like a church window. The matching steel hands of foliate diamond pattern look oddly heavy for the clock, but are original.

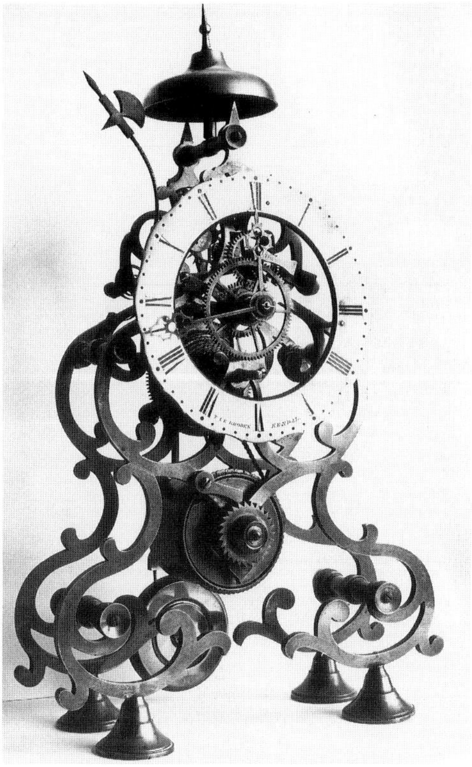

288. Single-fusee skeleton clock made about 1870 by T. & E. Rhodes of Kendal. Skeleton clocks were popular in the mid-nineteenth century, and originally each had a glass dome to keep out dust, though many have since lost them. The movement is exactly the same as a single train bracket clock (timepiece), with the exception that everything is open to view. All manner of ornate shapes were possible for the two skeletonized 'plates' which contained the movement, but many single-train examples had this sort of scrolled framework. Single-train skeleton clocks, such as this one, often strike a single blow at each hour, known as a passing strike, and this can be done by tripping a spring so that it does not draw driving power from the mainspring. The dial of this clock is a brass one with engraved numbers, but some have painted dials and some have skeletonized dials. This clock, like most others, has an anchor escapement.

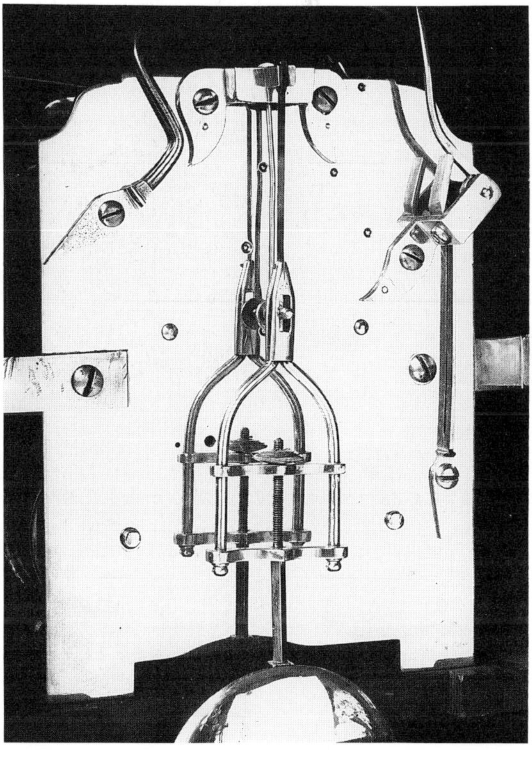

287. Backplate of the George Lee bracket clock (286) showing an interesting and unusual design for the pendulum, driven by an anchor escapement. Note the finely shaped tear drop ends to the attached work, the shaped shoulders to the clock plates and their stepped 'feet'. These are signs of quality of execution, as the clock would have functioned just as well with plain ones. The restraining straps are unusual in that the right-hand one attaches by a screw to the *inside* of the plate, whereas normal fitting is external like the left-hand one. In this instance the right-hand strap has been unconventionally positioned in order to avoid fouling the outside hammer spring.

5 *Spring wall clocks*

Spring-driven wall clocks appeared late on the British clockmaking scene; very few examples date from before the middle of the eighteenth century. This was probably because weight-driven wall clocks (such as lantern clocks, hook-and-spike clocks and hooded clocks) performed better as timekeepers, especially those with anchor escapement and long pendulum, and in addition the weight-driven ones were less delicate than spring clocks.

Virtually all spring-driven wall clocks were built with the fusee gear, on very similar principles to a bracket clock. Early ones originally had the verge escapement, but by the early nineteenth century most were made as anchor escapement. The great majority at all periods were timepieces only, that is had a single train and single fusee. Some had a second (striking) train, but these are unusual.

Various shapes of cases exist. The simplest have a narrow framework of circular outline, but some have a drop box beneath the circle, through a window in which the pendulum can be seen. Later examples, post-1830, may have a wider surround, veneered in mahogany or rosewood. Better examples were often inlaid with brass or sometimes with mother-of-pearl. Occasionally one is found made of papier mâché. Oak examples also exist, though these are often simpler and seldom have inlaid stringing.

Collectors recognize these clocks by a variety of different names. The commonest name is perhaps the English Dial Clock (even though by no means all were made in England). Round Dial Wall Clock, Fusee Wall Clock, Drop Dial Wall Clock and Drop Box Wall Clock are other names often used indiscriminately.

Some of these spring wall clocks drive on gutline, some on wire and some on tiny fusee chain. Chain is always thought of as being a superior feature, though of course it does not affect the running of the clock or its performance; it simply looks better.

Early examples had brass dials of the single-sheet type, engraved and silvered on the surface. Most however have japanned dials, similar to those on a round-dial longcase. Dial size was often 12 or 13 inches in diameter, except in Cartel clocks, where the dial was often quite small. Brass dials were generally on the small side, seldom exceeding 12 inches. Japanned dial examples less than 12 inches are thought more desirable; 10-inch examples or 8-inch ones being especially sought-after by collectors.

This same type of clock continued in manufacture, as Railway clocks for example, well into the 1940s. Some are lettered with the names of the railway companies, or the RAF, etc.

289. An English Cartel clock, the gilded frame made of carved wood. The frames are often ornate, as this one is, and of a similar nature to gilded mirrors. The Cartel clock is more often associated with France, where they were more numerous, and the frames were usually of ormolu or bronze. Cartel clocks are uncommon. This example was made by Storr & Gibbs of London and is actually dated 1741. The case is numbered XVII, though the casemaker is unknown. The movement is a timepiece with verge escapement and mock pendulum showing through the dial below XII. The blued steel hands are original, and not unlike those of a contemporary longcase or bracket clock. The dial is tiny, about 6 ins (15 cms) diameter, and is of silvered brass.

290. Movement of a single-train fusee wall clock with verge escapement, this particular one made about 1770 by Hedge of Colchester. This particular movement can be seen to have six pillars, which is an uncommonly high number. A high pillar count would usually be indicative of an early example of the type, as by the nineteenth century almost all have a standard four pillars. The picture shows well the bob pendulum (here at rest but not in its rest hook), the contrate and verge wheels, the verge pallets and the fusee itself. This movement is run on a wire cable. The dial feet can be seen pinned in place, exactly as on a longcase clock.

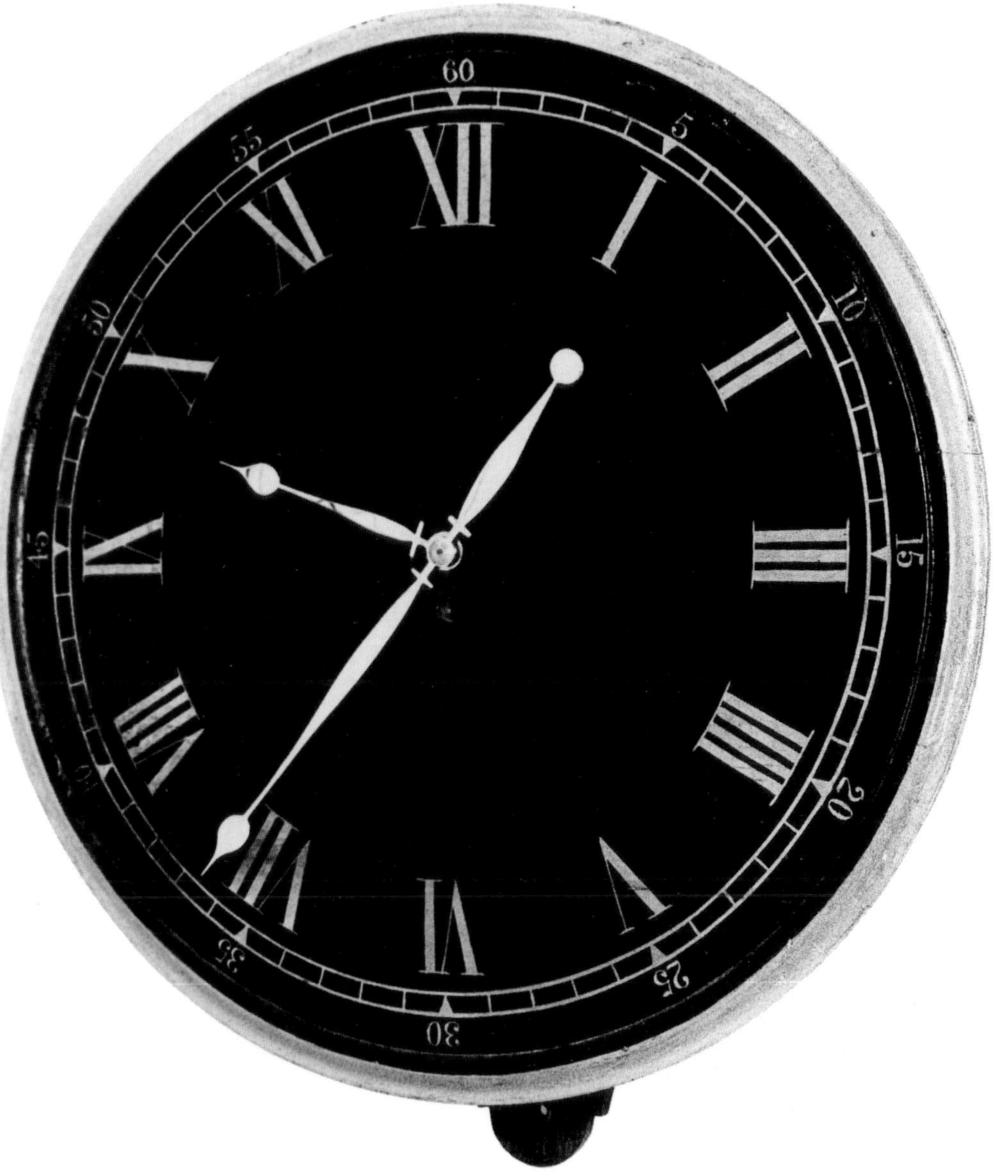

291. Black dial wall clock, the large dial (22 ins, 56 cms) being made of wood, painted black with gold numbering and edging. This is a spring-driven type of Tavern clock, probably made for use in a public building in the same way as a normal weight-driven Tavern clock, hence the exceptionally large dial. The original hands are of brass, the minute hand counter-balanced to avoid the drag which would otherwise result from its large size. Black-dial versions are uncommon. The movement has tapered plates (like many Tavern clocks), original verge escapement, and five pillars. These dials were made from joined planks, the boards usually separating with shrinkage over the years. The plank joints can be seen at thirteen minutes past and at twenty-three minutes past, where the shrink line also breaks the V numeral. The date is about 1770-80. This is a very unusual variant of a spring-driven wall clock.

292. Fusee wall clock with silvered brass dial and original verge escapement by William Ward of Bloomsbury, London, *c.* 1790. The single winding-hole indicates this is a timepiece only. The cutout below XII for a mock pendulum shows that this clock was built with verge escapement. The surround is in mahogany and the door has a cast brass bezel. The hour hand may well be original, but the minute hand is a much later replacement from a Victorian painted-dial longcase clock. The dial size is 12 ins (30.5 cms). Most of these verge-escapement brass-dial wall clocks were made in London, as indeed were the great majority of all fusee clocks. It is quite uncommon to find these clocks in original verge form today. The style varies little whether it bears a London or provincial maker's name.

293. Typical fusee wall clock of which many thousands were made. This is a timepiece dating from about 1830 with original blued steel hands. The case is in mahogany, and at this time the wooden surround was still narrow and restrained. Access for pendulum regulation is through a hinged door in the base, as with almost all these clocks. The makers, A. & G. Cairncross of Perth, are not recorded, and were probably retailers. The great majority of these clocks were London-made by specialists in this field, even though supplied ready-lettered with the name of the retailer. After about 1800 the numbering pattern remains static, with Roman hour numerals and no minute numbers. This dial is 11 ins (28 cms) in diameter. The escapement is of the anchor type, as were virtually all these clocks.

294. Single-fusee dial clock of the later, drop-box type, where the pendulum shows through the glass panel. This was made about 1850 by T.V. French of Newcastle upon Tyne, or at least was retailed by him. Shaped 'ears' join the circular surround to the vertical sides of the base, which was normal on this style of clock. The original hands are of blued steel. This clock is in rosewood, and by now the wider surround of wood was veneered on flat surfaces, including the chamfered flat rim. Such a shape was not made in solid wood on account of both the cost and the shrinkage problem. The escapement is an anchor. The dial size is 12 ins (30.5 cms). This style was often made of mahogany, though rosewood was especially popular in the 1840s. By this time oak was less often used, having been dropped in favour of more handsomely figured woods.

295. Single-fusee wall clock made about 1850. The name on the dial (Abraham Fawcett of Mirfield, Yorkshire) is probably that of the retailer rather than the actual maker. The octagonal case shape is often met with about this time, and was especially popular on American and German clocks which copied the English style, though they were usually two-train clocks and did not have fusees. The case is veneered in rosewood, and the inlay in this example is in mother-of-pearl, though brass inlay was often used. The hands are original, in blued steel, and typical of the period being relatively plain. The pendulum window is here cut in an ornate shape and edged with a brass quarter-round bead. This style would be referred to as an octagonal drop dial with pendulum window, to distinguish it from those without one. Dial size 12 ins (30.5 cms).

296. Single-fusee wall clock of the octagonal drop-box type made about 1850-60 and retailed by Charles Hodson of Worcester. This has a 12-inch (30.5 cms) dial. The unusual thing about this particular clock is that the case is made of papier mâché, set with mother-of-pearl pieces in clustered manner, like eggshell chippings. This is a very uncommon style, perhaps rather bright and glittery for most tastes. Here the drop-box section is formed integrally with the 'ears'; as the case is moulded anyway, the maker had no need to treat the 'ears' as separate sections to be joined on. The hands are of blued steel and are original. By this date the influx of imported clocks from America and Germany was creating havoc with the native clock trade. This showy style of case was perhaps one attempt at competing with imported work.

297. Large spring-driven fusee wall clock with painted wooden dial of about 24 ins (61 cms) diameter. This one has a pendant fitting at the top and probably hung down from some fixture in the manner of a department store clock. The clock has anchor escapement and a single fusee. It probably dates from the mid-nineteenth century, when wooden-dial clocks were very unusual. It was probably made as a one-off for a particular purpose. The name on the dial, M. McKenzie, tallies with that of a jeweller in Dingwall, Scotland, working in the 1860s. The dial is painted white. Both hands are counterbalanced against drag, and appear to be original, being of blued steel (the counterbalance ends are painted white). This clock probably acted as an advertising sign, perhaps in the doorway of McKenzie's shop, though under cover, as such a dial would not stand up to the weather.

298. A small drop-dial wall clock in an oak case dating from about 1880. The case shape with drop box and 'ears' is typical, though the swept base is not. However this clock is very small, the total height being only about 20 ins (50 cms). The dial is of silvered brass (an unusual feature as late as this) and is calibrated for twenty-four hours in engraved Roman numerals. Some owner has penned Arabic alternatives on the dial, presumably as they are less confusing. The retailer's name is Miller of Manchester, which is unrecorded. The clock bears an engraved plate reading 'Sidereal Time'. Oddly enough this covers a misspelt 'Sideral Time' engraved on the dial itself. Four screwheads hold the movement pillars to the dial. The movement is French with no fusee, so this was probably an English-made clock for a specific customer, built with a cheap imported movement. A sidereal day is roughly four minutes short of a normal mean time day of 24 hours (23 hours, 56 minutes, 4.09 seconds), and measures the time of one complete revolution of the earth relative to a star. Such a clock would be used primarily for astronomical observations.

299. View of a single-fusee spring-driven clock, this one being what is known as a Gallery clock, where the movement would be enclosed within a built-in box in the gallery of a chapel or public building. The japanned dial, seen only in profile on the right, is very large (24 ins, 61 cms). Winding and hand-setting are both carried out from the rear, here on the left of the photograph. The clock rests against an upright steel stand in this photograph. The anchor escapement shows clearly, as does the fusee chain and the long Victorian pinions. Bolts in the top two pillars were for some original fixing purpose. Note the very plain pillars. Makers Hopwood and Payne of Colchester, *c.* 1914-18. They were clockmakers, and this was probably an advertising clock for their shop doorway, under cover. It is of exceptionally heavy construction.

300. Twelve-inch (30.5 cms) japanned dial from a fusee wall clock of about 1840-50 by Wehrly & Co., Leeds, seen here removed from its movement and case during restoration. The movement pins to the dial by means of dial feet, just as with a longcase clock. Movement and dial are attached to the case by means of three screws through the dial rim (seen here at XII, IIII and VIII. Note the one at IIII has been re-positioned, probably because the screw had lost its grip in the wooden surround, as happens with repeated removal over the years for cleaning and repairing. The numbering pattern on these clocks is usually plain Roman hours, a style adopted after about 1810 and retained to the end of fusee clockmaking on wall clocks. This dial would have belonged to a school clock or something similar, but the dial would look no different in a costly brass-inlaid example for grander setting.

Glossary

Anchor: The anchor-shaped piece of an anchor escapement.
Apron: The brass cover, often decorative, which holds in place the knife-edge of a verge pendulum.
Arbor: The horological term for an axle.
Automata: Any moving figure on a clock dial, such as a rocking ship.
Back cock: The shaped brass fitting from which a pendulum hangs, particularly on a longcase clock.
Backplate: The rear plate of a plate-framed movement.
Balance-wheel: Single-spoked wheel used for regulating the speed of early lantern clocks.
Ball moon: Moon in the form of a sphere, turning to show moon phases.
Baluster pillar: Movement pillar of non-symmetrical shape.
Barrel: Drum on to which the gutline winds.
Birdcage: Alternative name for a posted movement.
Blind fret: A fret with a solid (wooden) backing.
Bluing: The process of colouring a clock hand by heating, usually on a bed of metal filings, to obtain a blue-black finish.
Bookmatched: A term used to indicate two or more pieces of veneer used side by side as a mirror-image.
Boss: Convex disc such as commonly used as a nameplate on a clock dial, usually in the arch area.
Bull's eye: The term often used to describe a bottle-glass as in the door of a longcase clock.
Bun feet: Round or ovoid wooden ball feet sometimes used on early longcase clocks or on bracket clocks.
Bush: Brass plug used to fill a worn pivot hole to re-centre a worn arbor.
Centre calendar: A feature whereby a clock shows the calendar from a hand pivoted at the same point as the hour and minute hands.
Centre seconds: A feature whereby a clock shows seconds from a long hand pivoted at the same point as the hour and minute hands.
Click: A pivoted stop-piece to prevent a wheel turning in reverse direction.
Collet: A brass ring by means of which a wheel is attached to its arbor. Also the brass washer by which clock hands are held tight, usually called a hands collet.

Contrate wheel: A wheel which changes the plane of turning of subsequent wheels in a train.
Countwheel: A wheel spaced at increasing intervals, usually by notches, to cause a clock to strike one blow more at every succeeding hour. Also known as a locking wheel or locking plate.
Crutch: A lever, usually forked at its tip, by means of which the clock's power is transmitted to a pendulum and through which most pendulums hang.
Deadbent escapement: A type of anchor escapement with no recoil, therefore beating 'dead'.
Dummy winders: Imitation winding-squares used on a thirty-hour clock to make it resemble superficially an eight-day one.
Dutch minute band: The name commonly given to a serpentine minute band sometimes seen in the mid-eighteenth century.
Ebonized: Stained with black polish to resemble ebony. A fine-grained wood such as pearwood was often used for this in bracket clocks; often pine in longcase clocks.
Falseplate: Iron fixing bracket supplied with a japanned dial to allow easier attachment of the movement.
Finial: Decorative terminal, of brass or gilded wood, as often used on the hoods of longcase clocks.
Flambeau: Term used to describe a certain type of finial, which represents a flaming torch.
Fly: A rotating vane used as an air brake to slow down the rate of striking of a clock.
Frontplate: The front plate of a plate-framed movement, that immediately behind the dial.
Fruitwood: General term used to describe the woods of certain fruit trees and used in cabinetmaking – such as plum, apple, pear, etc. Often used when it is impossible to determine which actual species was used.
Fusee: A cone-shaped intermediate gear. Its purpose is to reduce the varying pull of a spring when fully wound, against that when almost run down.
Gadroon (ed): Decorated with fluting or reeding, usually of tapering nature, such as that on the gadrooned chamfer top of a bracket clock case.
Half quarter (of an hour): That interval of time which divides a quarter of an hour equally (= 7½ minutes) and often marked on early two-handed clocks, namely at 7½ minutes past, 22½ minutes past, and the same time before the hour.
Halifax moon: A term often used ambiguously to mean either a moon-dial positioned below XII (either semi-circular or penny-shaped), or sometimes used to describe a penny-shaped moon in the arch of a clock dial. Sometimes misleadingly used to describe a ball moon.
Herringbone: In veneering a herringbone inlay is a chevron band

formed by two strips of veneer cut at an angle to each other, almost always is walnut. In engraving, a similar patterned edging usually around the outer edge of a dial sheet for decoration, when wheatear engraving is an alternative term.

Hook-and-spike: A term used to describe the way a clock hangs on the wall, supported from a hoop and distanced from the wall by spikes.

Hoop-and-spur: An alternative term for hook-and-spike.

Japanned: In clock casework this refers to a decorative process using gums and coloured paints. Also known as lacquer or chinoiserie. In clock dials this is the term for the process of decorating an iron sheet with a white ground and coloured decoration, as with white dials.

Kicking strip: The extreme lower mould on a clock case, which runs along the floor as an alternative to feet.

Knopped pillars: Pillars with a rounded raised section in the centre.

Latch: Latched pillars are held in place by swivel-pieces instead of the normal taper pins. Usually a feature of early clocks before about 1710.

Lenticle glass: The glass window in the trunk of a longcase clock, usually round, but occasionally of other shape.

Locking plate: Same thing as countwheel.

Maintaining power: A method of keeping a clock's wheels turning in drive during winding, usually by means of a spring, which comes into operation only during winding.

Matching hands: Hands where the minute hand is an elongated version of the same design as the hour hand.

Matted dial: Term used to describe the sandpaper-like finish of a clock dial centre. Sometimes known as frosting.

Mean time: The 24-hour daily time cycle as measured by most clocks in an attempt to average out solar time.

Moon dial: A sub-dial on a clock to show the moon's date and usually its shape (or phase). A lunar month has 29½ days without variation and is quite different from the calendar month.

Movement: The horological term for the works of a clock or watch.

One-piece dial: The term for a brass dial made from a single sheet of brass, not having separate added pieces such as a chapter ring. Also called a single-sheet dial.

Pallets: The faces of the escapement which come into contact with the escape wheel.

Patina: The deep surface sheen on long-waxed furniture.

Penny moon: A moon dial shaped as a circle and often about the size of an old penny.

Pillars: The posts which hold together the plates of a (plated) clock movement, commonly four in number and positioned towards the corners of the plates. On a posted movement the 'pillars' are known as posts.

Pinion: The smaller gears of steel which mesh into wheels.

Pivot: The narrowed end of an arbor, which turns within the plate and which takes the friction in drive.

Plate-frame: The type of movement where everything is contained between a front and back vertical plate.
Plinth: The lowest moulding strip on a longcase clock base, sometimes known as a kicking strip.
Posted movement: The type of movement construction where a top and bottom plate are held by posts, as with a lantern clock. Often known as a birdcage movement.
Pull-repeating: A repeating system which does not draw power from the clock's mainspring or driving weight, but in which the action of pulling charges a separate spring, which carries out the repeating function when released.
Rack striking: A system of striking which uses a rack and snail and enables the last hour to be repeated if desired.
Rating nut: The adjustion nut on a pendulum, usually at its base, to allow the clock to be set to a faster or slower pace.
Regulator: A master clock made by a clockmaker for his own use in testing his other clocks, often made with special features intended to give greater accuracy than a domestic clock. Some were also made to special order for customers who sought extra precision.
Rolling moon: The moon dial operating in the arch of a clock dial and normally filling the entire arch area.
Royal pendulum: Name sometimes given to the long pendulum (with anchor escapement).
Seat board: Wooden shelf on which a longcase movement sits when in its case.
Silvering: The treatment of parts of a brass dial (normally the engraved areas) with silver chloride paste sealed over with lacquer. This gave the dial a silver coating.
Single-sheet dial: Same as a one-piece dial.
Skeleton: A term used to indicate open parts between the solid. A skeleton clock has its plates pierced decoratively. A skeleton chapter ring has its brass cutaway to leave only the numbers.
Starwheel and jumper: A device designed to enable repeatingwork to function with greater accuracy.
Strawberry corners: A term used to indicate the flower-or-fruit style of corner painting as on the earliest period of white dials, whether or not actually featuring strawberries. Used mostly to indicate the period.
Stringing: Term describing inlay when in the form of lines; could be in wood or metal.
Swan-neck: The shaped curving 'horns' on a longcase clock hood.
Tic-tac escapement: A form of anchor escapement whereby the anchor spans very few teeth, commonly three teeth or less.
Tidal dial: A subdial to show times of high water, usually linked with the moon dial.
Timepiece: A non-striking clock.
Ting-tang: A form of chiming whereby the quarters are rung on two bells, playing one ting-tang at quarter past, two at half past, etc.

Train: A set of wheels, as e.g. a striking train.
Verre églomisé: A glass panel painted solid on the back and decoratively on the front. Used sometimes on the hoods of longcase clocks.
Wheatear engraving: Same as herringbone engraving.

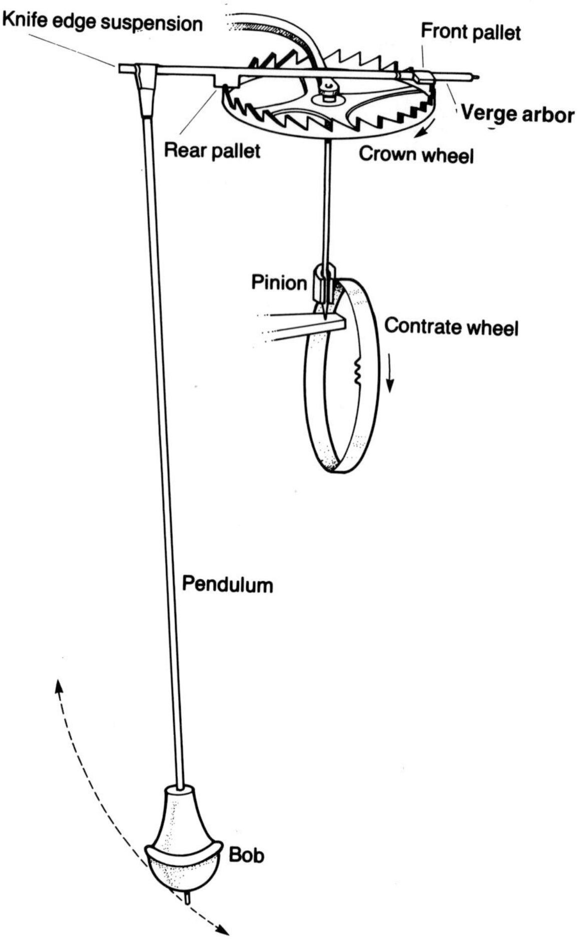

The principle of the verge escapement.

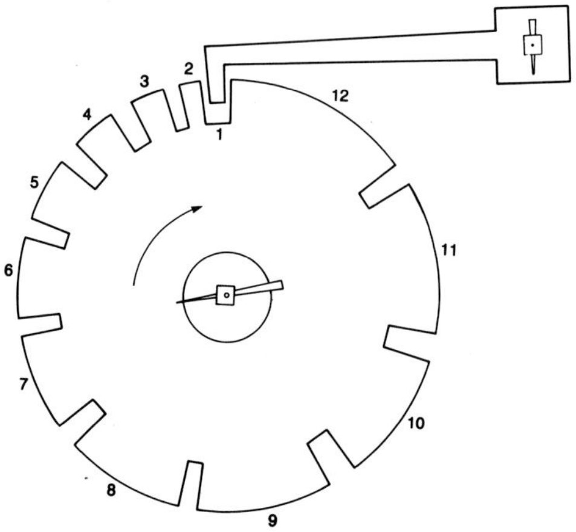

The principle of countwheel or locking-plate striking.

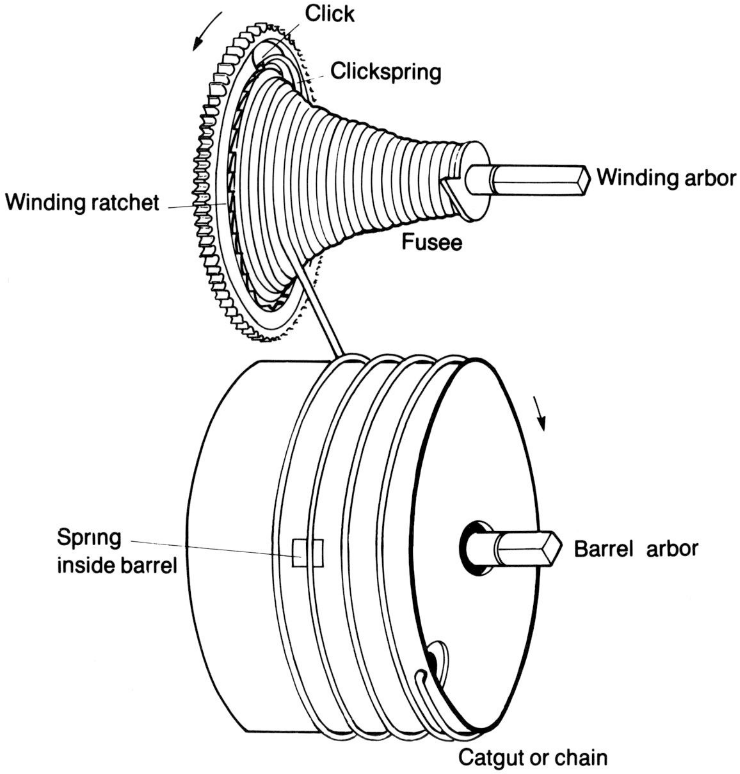

Above: The principle of the fusee. Arrows indicate direction during running.

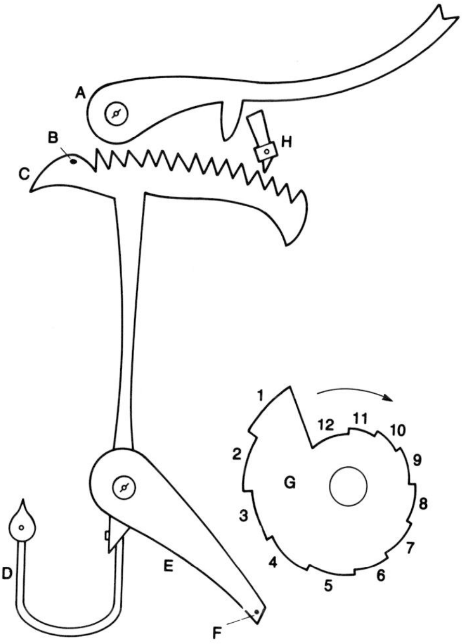

The principle of rack striking. The spring (D) pushes the rack (C) left so that the gathering pallet (H) can pick up the required number of teeth. A pin (F) on the rack tail(E) comes to rest against the stepped edge of the snail (G) offering the required count. The rack hook is (A). This system allows for the last hour to be repeated at will by means of a repeater trigger. (B) is a stop pin against which (H) comes to rest after the required count.

Select bibliography

Allan, Charles, *Old Stirling Clockmakers* (including St Ninians) (pub. privately, Stirling, 1990)

Baillie, G.H., *Watchmakers and Clockmakers of the World*, vol. 1 (NAG Press, 1976)

Barder, R.C.R., *English Country Grandfather Clocks* (David & Charles, 1983)

Barker, D., *The Arthur Negus Guide to Clocks* (Hamlyn, 1980)

Bates, Keith, *Clockmakers of Northumberland & Durham* (Pendulum Publications, 1980)

Beeson, C.F.C., *Clockmaking in Oxfordshire* (Museum of the History of Science, 1989)

Bellchambers, J.K., *Somerset Clockmakers* (Antiquarian Horological Society, 1968)

——, *Devonshire Clockmakers* (The Devonshire Press Ltd., 1962)

Britten, F.J., *Old Clocks & Watches* (Methuen, 9th ed., 1982)

Brown, H.M., *Cornish Clocks & Clockmakers* (David & Charles, 1970)

Bruton, Eric, *The Longcase Clock* (Hart-Davis, 1970)

——, *The Wetherfield Collection of Clocks* (NAG Press, 1981)

Daniel, John, *Leicestershire Clockmakers* (Leicestershire Museums, 1975)

Dawson, P., Drover, C.B., & Parkes, D.W., *Early English Clocks* (Antique Collectors' Club, 1982)

Dowler, Graham, *Gloucestershire Clock & Watch Makers* (Phillimore, 1984)

Edwardes, E.L., *The Grandfather Clock* (Sherrat, 1980)

——, *The Story of the Pendulum Clock*, (Sherrat, 1977)

Elliott, D.J., *Shropshire Clocks & Clockmakers* (Phillimore, 1979)

Haggar, A.L. & Miller, L.F., *Suffolk Clocks & Clockmakers* (Antiquarian Horological Society, 1974)

Hana, W.F.J., *English Lantern Clocks* (Blandford Press, 1979)

Hudson, Felix, *Scottish Clockmakers* (F. Hudson, Dunfermline, (?)1982)

Hughes, R.G., *Derbyshire Clock & Watch Makers* (Derby Museum, 1976)

Lee, R.A., *The Knibb Family Clockmakers* (Manor House Publications, 1963)

Legg, Edward, *Clock & Watchmakers of Buckinghamshire* (Bradwell Abbey Field Centre, 1976)

Lloyd, H. Alan, *Old Clocks* (Benn, 1958)

Loomes, Brian, *Antique British Clocks: A Buyer's Guide* (Robert Hale, 1991)

Loomes, Brian, *Complete British Clocks* (David & Charles, 1978)
——, *Country Clocks & their London Origins* (David & Charles, 1976)
——, *The Early Clockmakers of Great Britain* (NAG Press, 1982)
——, *Grandfather Clocks & their Cases* (David & Charles, 1985)
——, *Lancashire Clocks & Clockmakers* (David & Charles, 1975)
— *Watchmakers & Clockmakers of the World*, Vol. 2. (NAG Press, 1976, (revised 1989)
——, *Westmorland Clocks & Clockmakers* (David & Charles, 1974)
——, *White Dial Clocks, the Complete Guide* (David & Charles, 1981)
——, *Yorkshire Clockmakers* (George Kelsall, revised edition, 1985)
McKenna, Joseph, *Watch & Clockmakers of Warwickshire* (Pendulum Press, 1985)
——, *Watch & Clockmakers of Birmingham* (Pendulum Press, 1986)
Mason, Bernard, *Clock & Watch Making in Colchester* (Country Life, 1969)
Mather, H., *Clock & Watchmakers of Nottinghamshire* (The Friends of Nottingham Museum, 1979)
Moore, Nicholas, *Chester Clocks & Clockmakers* (Chester Museum, 1970s)
Norgate, J. & M., & Hudson, F., *Dunfermline Clockmakers* (F. Hudson, 1982)
Peate, I., *Clock & Watch Makers in Wales* (Welsh Folk Museum, 1960)
Penfold, John, *The Clockmakers of Cumberland* (Brant Wright Associates, 1977)
Penman, L., *The Clock Repairer's Handbook* (David & Charles/Arco, 1985)
Ponsford, Clive N., *Devon Clocks & Clockmakers* (David & Charles, 1985)
——, *Time in Exeter* (Headwell Vale Books, 1978)
——, & Authers, W.P., *Clocks & Clockmakers of Tiverton* (W.P. Authers, 1977)
Pryce, W.T.R., & Davies, T. Alun, *Samuel Roberts, Clockmaker* (Welsh Folk Museum, 1985)
Robinson, T., *The Longcase Clock* (Antique Collectors' Club, 1981)
Rose, Ronald E., *English Dial Clocks* (Antique Collectors' Club, 1978)
Royer-Collard, F.B., *Skeleton Clocks* (NAG Press, 1969)
Seaby, W.A., *Clockmakers of Warwick & Leamington* (Warwick Museum, 1981)
Smith, E., *Striking and Chiming Clocks* (David & Charles/Arco, 1985)
Smith, John, *Old Scottish Clockmakers* (E.P. Publishing Ltd., 1975)
Snell, Michael, *Clocks & Clockmakers of Salisbury* (Hobnob Press, 1986)
Symonds, R.W., *Thomas Tompion: his Life & Work* (Spring Books, 1968)
Tebbutt, Laurence, *Stamford Clocks and Watches* (Dolby Bros. Ltd., 1975)
Treherne, A.A., *Nantwich Clockmakers* (Nantwich Museum, (?) 1986)
Tribe, T., & Whatmoor, P., *Dorset Clocks & Clockmakers* (Tanat Books, 1981).
Tyler, E.J., *The Clockmakers of Sussex* (Watch & Clock Book Society, 1986)

Vernon, J., The Grandfather Clock Maintenance Manual (David & Charles/Van Nostrand Rheinhold, 1983)
Walker, J.E.S., *Hull & East Riding Clocks* (Hornsea Museum Publications, 1982)
Wallace, William, *Time in Hamilton* ((?) 1981)
White, George, *English Lantern Clocks* (Antique Collectors' Club, 1989)

Index

A-plates, 199
Abrahams, Lewis, 238
Act of Parliament clocks, 199
Agar, Mr, 134
American walnut, 140
Alarmwork, 33, 37, 45, 52, 64, 221
Anchor conversion, 208
Annual calendar, 137, 138, 193
Antram, Joseph, 220, 221
Apron, verge, 225
Arabic hours, 165, 166, 168, 170, 172, 175, 176, 177, 180, 181
Arched dial, 69, 214
Archer, Walter, 42, 43, 48, 49, 56
Architectural pediment, 156, 165
Ashwin & Co., 151
Aston, Edmund, 16
Astronomical dial, 137
Automata, see rocking figures

Balance wheel, 9
Ball moon, 120
Baluster pillars, 241
Bancroft, Mr, 180
Barber, Jonas, 124
Barleysugar pillars, 98, 99, 110
Barnsdale, John, 177
Barometer on dial, 144
Barron, John, 161
Barwise, Lot, 97, 140, 146
Basket top, 212
Bell, Edward, 157
Bewick, Thomas, 135
Black dial wall clock, 249
Blow, Henry, 186
Bob pendulum, 208
Bolton, John, 160
Bookmatched veneers, 99, 105, 109, 112, 116, 153, 163
Box top, 95
Bradford, Thomas, 30, 31, 101, 102
Braithwaite & Jones, 234
Brass, re-used, 15, 57
Brass dial, japanned later, 147
Break-arch hood, 137
Breakenrigg, J., 174
Brickwork base, 135
Brown, Henton, 38
——, John, 179
Bullock, Edmund, 110
Bunyan, Robert, 176
Burton, Emanuel, 96
——, William, 80, 81

Caddy top, 76, 80, 102, 107, 109, 114, 115, 117, 122
Cairncross A. & G., 251
Calendar, annual, 137, 138, 193
——, centre, 133, 162
Cameron, J., 194
Cartel clock, 247
Carved cases, 76, 95
Casemakers, 186, 189, 191
Casting faults, 25, 54, 219
Cawson, Mr, 183
Chamfer top, 236, 239
Chapman, William, 186
Cheasbrough, Aaron, 99
Chippendale sticks, 153
Chippendale style, 135, 226, 227, 228, 230, 231
Clare, Mr, 145
Clocksmiths, 45, 50
Coates, John, 128
Coats, J. & R., 163
Cock, William, 189
Coffin case, 73
Collier, David, 127
Cooper, Joseph, 103, 104, 105
Counterbalanced hands, 156, 160, 185, 201, 203, 249, 255
Countwheel striking, 21, 68, 87, 99
Coxeter, Nicholas, 15
Crampton, John, 218, 219
Croome, Robert, 60
Cruttenden, Thomas, 212, 213

Dammant, Barnaby, 222
Dated clocks, 13, 23, 99, 125, 169, 178, 204, 214, 233, 247

Davenport, William, 122
Davidson, James, 195
Daws, Thomas, 202
Deacon, Samuel, 165, 169
De Charmes, Simon, 32
Delaunce, James, 22
Dials, enamel, 150
——, single-sheet, see single-sheet dials
——, sizes, 69
Dotted minutes, 138, 143, 148, 150, 152, 162
Drop box, 245, 252, 253, 254
Drury, William, 91
Dummy winding holes/squares, 77, 84, 86, 89, 93
Dutch minute band, 90, 124, 128

Earpieces, 202, 203, 252, 254
Ebony/ebonized, 97, 98, 208
Eggert, D., 166, 167
Egyptian influence, 236
Elm, 85
Enamel dial, 150
Engraving, backplates, 211, 213, 215, 217, 219, 223, 233
——, practice, 22, 42
Equation of Time, 137
Esplin, George, 190
Ettry, John, 123

Falseplates, 70, 151, 159, 167
Farquharson, R.W., 197
Farrar, Abraham, 28, 29
——, William, 106, 214, 215
Fawcett, Abraham, 253
Fearnley, Peter, 139
Fecit, use of, 106, 211
Feet, front only, 137
Felton, Thomas, 168
Ferris, James, 237
Field, Thomas, 143
Fisher, Henry, 93
Flower, Robert, 79
Fly dial, 172
Foster, James, 158
Four seasons, 90, 170, 194, 197
Francis, Richard, 204
French feet, 174
French, T.V., 252
Frodsham, Mr, 235
Fruitwood, 98
Fuller, Robert, 155
Fusee, 222, 245, 257
Fusee conversion (lanterns), 22, 27

Gallery clock, 257
Ganter, Paul, 196
Garland, Edward, 171
Gerrans, F.C., 232, 233
Gerrard, John, 217
Gillows, 156, 183
Girod, James, 100
Gothic door, 153, 171, 195
Green, John, 226, 227
——, Peter, 116
Greening, Benjamin, 185
Griffith, Rowland, 151
Guest, George, 20

Hackett, Richard, 133
Half-quarters, 52, 101
Hammond, G., 239
Handscomb, Ebenezer, 92
Hardaker, Mr, 147
Hargraves, Thomas, 148
——, William, 86
Hedge, Mr, 248
Henderson, Robert, 84
Herringbone engraving, 101, 103, 104, 108, 113, 115, 216, 217
Hodson, Charles, 254
Holmes, John, 154
Hooded clocks, 11, 58, 59, 60, 61, 62, 63, 64, 65
Hood side windows, 100, 103, 106, 109, 115, 118, 131, 159, 184
Hook-and-spike clocks, 11, 42, 44, 46, 48, 50
Hopwood & Payne, 257
Howe & Knox, 136
Humphries, William, 46

Iron bellstrap, 25, 28
Iron pillars, 83
Ivory, James, 130, 131

Jackson, John, 183
Japanned dial (over brass), 147
Japanning, woodwork, 208, 223
Jones, Mr, 56

King, Mr, 241
——, Peter, 107, 108, 109
Knibb, John, 211
Knifton, Thomas, 18
Knowles, Andrew, 113

Lacquer casework, 102, 111, 223
Lancet clock, 237
Lantern clocks, 9
——, arched dial, 36, 38, 41
——, miniature, 32, 33, 36
——, square dial, 35
Latches/latched pillars, 98
Latinized signatures, 215
Lawrie, Archibald, 135
Lee, George, 242, 243
Leeds case style, 137
Lenticle glass 78, 79, 98, 99, 102, 103, 105, 110, 123

Lister, Thomas, 94, 95, 230, 231
——, William, 138
Locking plate, see countwheel
Lovelace, Jacob, 112

McKenzie, M., 255
McMasters, Samuel, 181
Marquetry, 100, 107
Marriage clocks, 23, 125, 140
Martin, Richard, 27
Mason, John, 35
Matting of dials, 54, 81, 85, 88, 89, 126, 136
Mawkes, Thomas, 182
Mayhew, Henry, 34
Medullary rays 110, 123, 177
Miles, George, 90
Miller, Mr, 256
Mills, Humfrey, 17
Mock pendulum, 216, 217, 228
Month clock, 100
Moon dials, ball, 120
——, half-circle, 94
——, others, see under name
Mortimore, Mr, 178
Moseley, Joshua, 82, 83
Moss, Thomas, 229
Murray, William, 193
Musical clocks, 87, 112, 120, 121

Nicholas, W. & C., 150
——, William, 170, 171
Norfolk clock, 200, 204, 205
Numbered clocks, 81, 110, 124, 169

Oak, quarter-cut, 92, 123, 132, 149
——, slash-sawn, 92, 198
Ogden, James, 24, 28
——, Thomas, 117
One-piece dial, see single-sheet dial
Osborne & Wilson, 70, 146, 149
Owners' names, 23, 26, 140

Pagoda top, 131, 134, 164
Papier mâché, 254
Parratt, Samuel, 85
Passing strike, 104, 243
Peckover, Richard, 40
Penny moon, 80, 82, 110, 117, 126
Pillars attached, 83
——, number of, 98, 101, 219, 222, 248
Pinney, Mr, 191
Pin-wheel escapement, 231
Plated movement, 67
Porthouse, William, 125
Posted movement, 67
Potts, Joseph, 162, 163
Prices, original, 70, 165
Pull-repeating, 209, 211, 216, 218, 219, 221, 223

Quarter-chiming, 73, 104, 171, 173, 224, 225, 241
Quarter-cut oak, 92, 123, 132, 149
Quartering (bookmatching), 109

Rack striking, 141, 233, 241
Radford, Thomas, 142
Raymond, Charles, 62
Raynes, William, 19
Red walnut, 140
Regulator, 96, 145
Repeating work, 207, 239
Rhodes, T. & E., 243
Ringed winding holes, 101, 103, 104, 108
Rising hood, 73
Rivets in dial, 82, 86, 88, 94, 117
Rocking figures, 81, 93, 110, 128, 158, 177, 190
Rolling eyes, 81
Rolling moon, 113, 124, 127
Rope-twist columns, 184, 185, 189, 198
Rosewood, 234, 238, 252, 253
Round dials, 134, 154
Rudd, Edward, 129
Rule, James, 144

Sanderson, John, 52, 111, 216
Savage, Richard, 23
Screws in dial, 144
Scholfield, Major, 153
Seconds, centre, 133
Selwood, William, 14
Shakeshaft, Lawrence, 156
Shaw, William, 41
Shield dial, 201
Sidereal time, 256
Single-handed clocks, 68
Single-sheet dials, 62, 64, 90, 96, 134, 143, 144, 145, 228, 229, 230, 245, 250
Six-month clock, 185
Skeleton clock, 243
Smith, James, 184
——, John, 172, 173
——, T., 63
Snail, 141, 241
Snow, Richard, 192
Spandrels, absence of, 52, 54, 84
Spendlove, John, 175
Springs, 207
Split-trains verge, 15, 25, 29, 31, 41
Stamper, Francis, 21
Starburst, 117, 118
Starwheel, 233
Stepped plates, 83
Sterling, Mr, 64, 65
Stevens, Edward, 228
Stobo, Thomas, 159
Stockton, Thomas, 89
Stokes, J., 188

Storr & Gibbs, 247
Strawberry corners, 153, 161
Strike/silent, 130
Stumbels, William, 115, 120, 121
Sunrise/sunset dials, 137, 193
Swan-neck feature, 136, 143, 157, 167, 173, 175, 181, 183
Sweep seconds, 133

Tantum, Daniel, 118, 119
Tavern clock (spring), 249
Taylor, Mr, 240
——, John, 114
Thorpe, Mr, 189
Tic-tac escapement, 49
Tidal dials, 115, 120, 124, 133, 172
Timepiece, 245
Ting-tang striking, 231, 241
Tortoiseshell, 214
Trains, multiple, 68, 90, 120, 122, 171, 173, 199, 204, 205
Tudor Rose, 15, 25, 26, 46, 56, 74
Turkish market clocks, 38, 40
Twenty-four-hour dial, 160

Unsigned clocks, 44, 50, 54, 58, 59, 61, 75
Utting, Thomas, 223

Verge escapement, on lantern clocks, 10, 21, 23, 29, 31, 33, 39, 41, 65
——, on bracket clocks, 208, 211
——, on wall clocks, 245, 247, 248
Verre églomisé, 116, 139, 163
Verses on dials, 52, 111

Waggitt, Michael, 88
Waklin, John, 74
Wallen, William, 132
Walnut, American (i.e. red), 140
Ward, H., 198
——, William, 250
Waren, William, 149
Webster, William, 36
Wedding clocks, 23, 125, 140
Wehrly & Co., 258
Whale tail cresting, 155
Wheatear, see herringbone
White dials, 70
White, Joseph, 224, 225
Whittaker, Samuel, 76
Wilcox, J., 191
Wilkinson, William, 137
Williamson, John, 73
Wilson, James 126, 152, 157, 161, 166, 167, 172
Winding squares, fancy, 135
Wise, John, 98
Wolley, James, 77
Wood, F., 187
World time dial, 122, 160
Wreghit, John, 164
Wright, John, 203

Yeomans, Mr, 236

Zig-zag dials, 50